baking

100 everyday recipes

First published in 2011
LOVE FOOD is an imprint of Parragon Books Ltd

Parragon
Chartist House
15-17 Trim Street
Bath BA1 1HA, UK
www.parragon.com

ISBN: 978-1-4454-3039-3

Printed in China

Produced by Ivy Contract
Photography by Charlie Paul

Notes for the Reader

This book uses both metric and imperial measurements. Follow the same units of measurement throughout; do not mix metric and imperial. All spoon measurements are level: teaspoons are assumed to be 5 ml, and tablespoons are assumed to be 15 ml. Unless otherwise stated, milk is assumed to be full fat, eggs and individual vegetables are medium, and pepper is freshly ground black pepper.

The times given are an approximate guide only. Preparation times differ according to the techniques used by different people and the cooking times may also vary from those given. Optional ingredients, variations or serving suggestions have not been included in the calculations.

Recipes using raw or very lightly cooked eggs should be avoided by infants, the elderly, pregnant women, convalescents and anyone suffering from an illness. Pregnant and breastfeeding women are advised to avoid eating peanuts and peanut products. Sufferers from nut allergies should be aware that some of the ready-made ingredients used in the recipes in this book may contain nuts. Always check the packaging before use.

baking

introduction

Baking is without any doubt the most rewarding of culinary experiences. To mix together the most unpromising-looking collection of ingredients, put them in an oven and have them emerge as a truly delicious creation is nothing short of a miracle!

No wonder, then, that there is something of a mystery to the whole process that is often daunting to an inexperienced cook. In reality, however, it's nowhere near as difficult as it might appear to bake a sumptuous large cake, a melt-in-the-mouth muffin, your favourite pie, a loaf of bread to serve fresh from the oven or an elegant savoury tart – and these are just a few examples of the wonderful baking recipes you will find in this book.

There are several items of kitchen equipment that are worth investing in if you are planning to make baking a regular event. A selection of baking tins is a must – baking sheets and tart tins, as well as round and square cake tins of various sizes, including one or two of the 'springform' type to facilitate the removal of large cakes, tortes and cheesecakes.

Apart from this, a couple of generously sized mixing bowls, some wooden spoons and perhaps a hand-held electric mixer will be enough to get you started. A more expensive item of equipment that will pay for itself in no time is a multipurpose food mixer. The different attachments will enable you to mix cake batters and pastry, whisk egg whites, whip cream and knead bread dough with speed and efficiency. In the past, of course, cooks had no such gadgets to help them out, and there is a certain satisfaction in doing all of the above tasks by hand – kneading bread dough for ten minutes is guaranteed to relieve tension as well as produce a fabulous result.

Choose your favourite recipe, mix it with confidence, bake it until it is prefect and wait for the golden moment when you can bite into it!

cakes & gâteaux

coffee & walnut cake

ingredients

serves 8

175 g/6 oz unsalted butter,
    plus extra for greasing
175 g/6 oz light muscovado sugar
3 large eggs, beaten
3 tbsp strong black coffee
175 g/6 oz self-raising flour
1½ tsp baking powder
115 g/4 oz walnut pieces
walnut halves, to decorate

frosting

115 g/4 oz unsalted butter
200 g/7 oz icing sugar
1 tbsp strong black coffee
½ tsp vanilla extract

method

1 Grease and line the bases of two 20-cm/8-inch sandwich tins.

2 Cream together the butter and muscovado sugar until pale and fluffy. Gradually add the eggs, beating well after each addition. Beat in the coffee.

3 Sift the flour and baking powder into the mixture, then fold in lightly and evenly with a metal spoon. Fold in the walnut pieces.

4 Divide the mixture between the prepared cake tins and smooth level. Bake in a preheated oven, 180°C/350°F/Gas Mark 4, for 20–25 minutes, or until golden brown and springy to the touch. Turn out onto a wire rack to cool.

5 For the frosting, beat together the butter, icing sugar, coffee and vanilla extract, mixing until smooth and creamy.

6 Use about half the mixture to sandwich the cakes together, then spread the remaining frosting on top and swirl with a palette knife. Decorate with walnut halves.

hummingbird cake

ingredients

serves 10

250 g/9 oz plain flour
250 g/9 oz caster sugar
1 tbsp ground cinnamon
1 tbsp bicarbonate of soda
3 eggs, beaten
200 ml/7 fl oz sunflower oil, plus
    extra for greasing
100g/3½ oz pecan nuts, roughly
    chopped, plus extra to decorate
3 ripe bananas (about 375 g/13 oz
    peeled weight), mashed
85 g/3 oz canned crushed
    pineapple (drained weight),
    plus 4 tbsp from the can

frosting

175 g/6 oz full-fat soft cheese
55g/2 oz unsalted butter
400g/14 oz icing sugar

method

1 Lightly grease three 23-cm/9-inch sandwich tins with oil and line the bases with baking paper.

2 Sift together the flour, caster sugar, cinnamon and bicarbonate of soda into a large bowl. Add the eggs, oil, pecan nuts, bananas, pineapple and pineapple juice, and stir with a wooden spoon until evenly mixed.

3 Divide the mixture between the prepared tins, spreading evenly. Bake in a preheated oven, 180°C/ 350°F/Gas Mark 4, for 20–25 minutes, or until golden brown and firm to the touch.

4 Remove the cakes from the oven and leave to cool for 10 minutes in the tins before turning out onto wire racks and allowing to cool completely.

5 For the frosting, beat together the soft cheese, butter and vanilla extract in a bowl until smooth. Sift in the icing sugar and mix until smooth.

6 Sandwich the cakes together with half of the frosting, spread the remaining frosting over the top, then sprinkle with pecan nuts to decorate.

madeira cake

ingredients

serves 8–10

175 g/6 oz unsalted butter,
    plus extra for greasing
175 g/6 oz caster sugar
finely grated rind of 1 lemon
3 large eggs, beaten
115 g/4 oz plain flour
115 g/4 oz self-raising flour
2–3 tbsp brandy or milk
2 slices of citron peel

method

1 Grease and line an 18-cm/7-inch round deep cake tin.

2 Cream together the butter and sugar until pale and fluffy. Add the lemon rind and gradually beat in the eggs. Sift in the flours and fold in evenly, adding enough brandy to make a soft dropping consistency.

3 Spoon the mixture into the prepared tin and smooth the surface. Lay the slices of citron peel on top of the cake.

4 Bake in a preheated oven, 160°C/325°F/Gas Mark 3, for 1–1¼ hours, or until well risen, golden brown and springy to the touch.

5 Cool in the tin for 10 minutes, then turn out and cool completely on a wire rack.

red velvet cake

ingredients

serves 12

225 g/8 oz unsalted butter,
    plus extra for greasing
4 tbsp water
55 g/2 oz cocoa powder
3 eggs
250 ml/9 fl oz buttermilk
2 tsp vanilla extract
2 tbsp red edible food colouring
280 g/10 oz plain flour
55 g/2 oz cornflour
1½ tsp baking powder
280 g/10 oz caster sugar

frosting

250 g/9 oz full-fat soft cheese
40 g/1½ oz unsalted butter
3 tbsp caster sugar
1 tsp vanilla extract

method

1 Grease two 23-cm/9-inch sandwich tins and line the bases with baking paper. Place the butter, water and cocoa powder in a small saucepan and heat gently, without boiling, stirring until melted and smooth. Remove from the heat and cool.

2 Beat together the eggs, buttermilk, vanilla extract and food colouring until frothy. Beat in the butter mixture. Sift together the flour, cornflour and baking powder, then stir into the mixture with the caster sugar.

3 Divide the mixture between the prepared tins and bake in a preheated oven, 190°C/375°F/Gas Mark 5, for 25–30 minutes, or until risen and firm to the touch. Leave to cool in the tins for 3–4 minutes. Turn out and finish cooling on a wire rack.

4 For the frosting, beat together all the ingredients until smooth. Use about half of the frosting to sandwich the cakes together, then spread the remainder over the top, swirling with a palette knife.

variation

If you prefer not to use food colouring, use 4 tablespoons of beetroot juice with 2 tablespoons of water. With an electric juicer, 1 medium beetroot should yield about 4 tablespoons of juice.

orange & poppy seed bundt cake

ingredients

serves 10

200 g/7 oz unsalted butter,
    plus extra for greasing
200 g/7 oz golden caster sugar
3 large eggs, beaten
finely grated rind of 1 orange
55 g/2 oz poppy seeds
300 g/10½ oz plain flour, plus extra
    for dusting
2 tsp baking powder
150 ml/5 fl oz milk
125 ml/4 fl oz orange juice
strips of orange zest, to decorate

syrup

140 g/5 oz golden caster sugar
150 ml/5 fl oz orange juice

method

1 Grease and lightly flour a Bundt ring tin, about
   24 cm/9 inches in diameter and with a capacity of
   approximately 2 litres/3 pints.

2 Cream together the butter and sugar until pale and
   fluffy, then add the eggs gradually, beating thoroughly
   after each addition. Stir in the orange rind and poppy
   seeds. Sift in the flour and baking powder, then fold
   in evenly. Add the milk and orange juice, stirring to
   mix evenly.

3 Spoon the mixture into the prepared tin and bake in
   a preheated oven, 160°C/325°F/Gas Mark 3, for 45–50
   minutes, or until firm and golden brown. Leave to cool
   in the tin for 10 minutes, then turn out onto a wire rack
   to cool.

4 For the syrup, place the sugar and orange juice in a
   saucepan and heat gently until the sugar melts. Bring
   to the boil and simmer for about 5 minutes, until
   reduced and syrupy.

5 Spoon the syrup over the cake whilst it is still warm.
   Top with the strips of orange zest and serve warm
   or cold.

birthday lemon sponge cake

ingredients

serves 8–10

sponge

250 g/9 oz unsalted butter,
    plus extra for greasing
250 g/9 oz golden caster sugar
4 eggs, beaten
250 g/9 oz self-raising flour
finely grated rind of 1 lemon
3 tbsp milk

butter icing

140 g/5 oz unsalted butter
200 g/7 oz icing sugar
2 tbsp lemon juice or lemon
    liqueur (Limoncello)
3 tbsp lemon curd

method

1 Grease two 20-cm/8-inch sandwich tins and line the bases with baking paper.

2 Cream together the butter and caster sugar until pale and fluffy. Gradually add the eggs, beating well after each addition. Sift in the flour and fold in evenly with a metal spoon. Fold in the lemon rind and milk lightly and evenly.

3 Spoon the mixture into the prepared tins and bake in a preheated oven, 180°C/350°F/Gas Mark 4, for 25–30 minutes, or until golden brown and springy to the touch. Leave the cakes to cool in the tins for 2–3 minutes, then turn out onto a wire rack to finish cooling.

4 For the butter icing, beat together the butter, icing sugar and lemon juice until smooth. Mix about 3 tablespoons of the butter cream with the lemon curd. Use the lemon curd mixture to sandwich the two cakes together.

5 Spread about two thirds of the remaining butter icing over the top of the cake, swirling with a palette knife. Spoon the remainder into a piping bag and pipe swirls around the edge of the cake. Add candleholders and birthday candles to finish.

chocolate fudge cake

ingredients

serves 8

175 g/6 oz unsalted butter,
    softened, plus extra
    for greasing
175 g/6 oz golden caster sugar
3 eggs, beaten
3 tbsp golden syrup
40 g/1½ oz ground almonds
175 g/6 oz self-raising flour
pinch of salt
40 g/1½ oz cocoa powder

icing

225 g/8 oz plain chocolate,
    broken into pieces
55 g/2 oz dark muscovado sugar
225 g/8 oz unsalted butter, diced
5 tbsp evaporated milk
½ tsp vanilla extract

method

1 Grease and line the bottom of 2 x 20-cm/8-inch round
   cake tins. To make the icing, place the chocolate,
   sugar, butter, evaporated milk and vanilla extract in a
   heavy-based pan. Heat gently, stirring constantly, until
   melted. Pour into a bowl and cool. Cover and chill in
   the refrigerator for 1 hour, or until spreadable.

2 Place the butter and sugar in a bowl and beat together
   until light and fluffy. Gradually beat in the eggs. Stir in
   the syrup and ground almonds. Sift the flour, salt and
   cocoa into a separate bowl, then fold into the mixture.
   Add a little water, if necessary, to make a dropping
   consistency. Spoon the mixture into the prepared tins
   and bake in a preheated oven, 180°C/350°F/Gas Mark 4,
   for 30–35 minutes, or until springy to the touch and a
   skewer inserted in the centre comes out clean.

3 Leave the cakes in the tins for 5 minutes, then turn
   out onto wire racks to cool completely. When the cakes
   are cold, sandwich them together with half the icing.
   Spread the remaining icing over the top and sides of
   the cake, swirling it to give a frosted appearance.

carrot cake

ingredients

serves 16

2 eggs
175 g/6 oz molasses sugar
200 ml/7 fl oz sunflower oil
200 g/7 oz coarsely grated carrots
225 g/8 oz wholemeal flour
1 tsp baking soda
2 tsp ground cinnamon
whole nutmeg, grated
    (about 1 tsp)
115 g/4 oz roughly chopped
    walnuts

topping

115 g/4 oz half-fat
    cream cheese
4 tbsp butter, softened
85 g/3 oz icing sugar
1 tsp grated lemon rind
1 tsp grated orange rind

method

1 In a mixing bowl, beat the eggs until well blended and add the sugar and oil. Mix well. Add the grated carrot, sift in the flour, baking soda and spices, then add the walnuts. Mix everything together until well incorporated.

2 Grease and line a 20-cm/8-inch round cake tin. Spread the mixture into the prepared cake tin and bake in the centre of a preheated oven, 190°C/375°F/Gas Mark 5, for 40–50 minutes until the cake is nicely risen, firm to the touch and has begun to shrink away slightly from the edge of the tin. Remove from the oven and cool in the tin until just warm, then turn out onto a cooling rack.

3 To make the topping, put all the ingredients into a mixing bowl and beat together for 2–3 minutes until really smooth.

4 When the cake is completely cold, spread with the topping, smooth over with a fork, and allow to firm up a little before cutting into 16 portions. Store in an airtight container in a cool place for up to 1 week.

sponge cake

ingredients

serves 8–10

175 g/6 oz butter, at room
	temperature, plus extra
	for greasing
175 g/6 oz caster sugar
3 eggs, beaten
175 g/6 oz self-raising flour
pinch of salt

to serve

3 tbsp raspberry jam
1 tbsp caster or icing sugar

method

1 Grease 2 x 20-cm/8-inch round sponge cake tins and
base-line with baking paper.

2 Beat the butter and sugar together in a mixing bowl
using a wooden spoon or a hand-held mixer until the
mixture is pale in colour and light and fluffy. Add the
egg a little at a time, beating well after each addition.

3 Sift the flour and salt and carefully add to the mixture,
folding it in with a metal spoon or a spatula. Divide the
mixture between the tins and smooth over with the
spatula. Place them on the same shelf in the centre of
a preheated oven, 180°C/350°F/Gas Mark 4, and bake
for 25–30 minutes until well risen, golden brown and
beginning to shrink from the sides of the tins.

4 Remove from the oven and let stand for 1 minute.
Loosen the cakes from around the edge of the tins
using a round-bladed knife. Turn the cakes out onto
a clean tea towel, remove the paper and invert them
onto a wire rack (this prevents the wire rack from
marking the top of the cakes). When completely cool,
sandwich together with the jam and sprinkle with
the sugar.

sticky ginger marmalade loaf

ingredients

serves 10

175 g/6 oz butter, softened, plus
    extra for greasing
125 g/4½ oz ginger marmalade
175 g/6 oz brown sugar
3 eggs, beaten
225 g/8 oz self-raising flour
½ tsp baking powder
1 tsp ground ginger
100 g/3½ oz coarsely
    chopped pecans

method

1 Grease and line the bottom and ends of a 900-g/2-lb loaf tin. Place 1 tablespoon of the ginger marmalade in a small pan and reserve. Place the remaining marmalade in a bowl with the butter, sugar and eggs.

2 Sift in the flour, baking powder and ground ginger and beat together until smooth. Stir in three-quarters of the nuts. Spoon the mixture into the prepared loaf tin and smooth the top. Sprinkle with the remaining nuts and bake in a preheated oven, 180°C/350°F/Gas Mark 4, for 1 hour, or until well risen and a skewer inserted into the centre comes out clean.

3 Cool in the tin for 10 minutes, then turn out and peel off the lining paper. Transfer to a wire rack to cool slightly. Set the pan of reserved marmalade over low heat to warm, then brush over the loaf and serve in slices.

variation

For something different, replace the coarsely chopped pecans with 100 g/3½ oz coarsely chopped macadamia nuts or walnuts.

date & walnut loaf

ingredients

serves 10

175 g/6 oz butter, plus extra
    for greasing
225 g/8 oz pitted dates, chopped
    into small pieces
grated rind and juice of 1 orange
50 ml/2 fl oz water
175 g/6 oz brown sugar
3 eggs, beaten
85 g/3 oz wholemeal
    self-raising flour
85 g/3 oz self-raising flour
55 g/2 oz chopped walnuts
8 walnut halves
orange zest, to decorate

method

1 Grease and line the bottom and ends of a 900-g/2-lb loaf tin. Place the dates in a pan with the orange rind and juice and water and cook over medium heat for 5 minutes, stirring, or until a soft purée has formed.

2 Place the butter and sugar in a bowl and beat together until light and fluffy. Gradually beat in the eggs, then sift in the flours and fold in with the chopped walnuts. Spread one-third of the mixture over the bottom of the prepared loaf tin and spread half the date purée over the top.

3 Repeat the layers, ending with the cake mixture. Arrange walnut halves on top. Bake in a preheated oven, 160°C/325°F/Gas Mark 3, for 1–1¼ hours, or until well risen and firm to the touch. Cool in the tin for 10 minutes. Turn out, peel off the lining paper and transfer to a wire rack to cool. Decorate with orange zest and serve in slices.

gingerbread

ingredients

serves 12–16

450 g/1 lb plain flour
3 tsp baking powder
1 tsp baking soda
3 tsp ground ginger
175 g/6 oz butter
175 g/6 oz soft brown sugar
175 g/6 oz black molasses
175 g/6 oz golden syrup
1 egg, beaten
300 ml/10 fl oz milk

method

1 Line a 23-cm/9-inch square cake tin, 5 cm/2 inches deep, with baking paper.

2 Sift the flour, baking powder, baking soda and ginger into a large mixing bowl.

3 Place the butter, sugar, molasses and syrup in a medium pan and heat over low heat until the butter has melted and the sugar dissolved. Cool a little.

4 Mix the beaten egg with the milk and add to the cooled syrup mixture. Add the liquid ingredients to the flour mixture and beat well using a wooden spoon until the mixture is smooth and glossy.

5 Pour the mixture into the prepared tin and bake in the centre of a preheated oven, 160°C/325°F/Gas Mark 3, for 1½ hours until well risen and just firm to the touch.

6 Remove from the oven and cool in the tin. When cool, remove the cake from the tin with the lining paper. Overwrap with foil and place in an airtight container for up to 1 week to allow the flavours to mature. Cut into wedges to serve.

torta de cielo

ingredients

serves 4–6

225 g/8 oz unsalted butter, at
   room temperature, plus extra
   for greasing
175 g/6 oz whole almonds,
   in their skins
225 g/8 oz sugar
3 eggs, lightly beaten
1 tsp almond extract
1 tsp vanilla extract
9 tbsp plain flour
pinch of salt

to decorate

icing sugar, for dusting
slivered almonds, toasted

method

1 Lightly grease a 20-cm/8-inch round cake tin and line
   the tin with baking paper.

2 Place the almonds in a food processor and process
   to form a 'mealy' mixture. Set aside.

3 Beat the butter and sugar together in a large bowl until
   smooth and fluffy. Beat in the eggs, almonds and both
   the almond and vanilla extracts until well blended.
   Stir in the flour and salt and mix briefly, until the flour
   is just incorporated.

4 Pour or spoon the batter into the prepared tin and
   smooth the surface. Bake in a preheated oven,
   180°C/350°F/Gas Mark 4, for 40–50 minutes, or until
   the cake feels spongy when gently pressed.

5 Remove from the oven and cool on a wire rack. To
   serve, dust with icing sugar and decorate with toasted
   slivered almonds.

chocolate truffle torte

ingredients

serves 10

butter, for greasing
55 g/2 oz golden caster sugar
2 eggs
25 g/1 oz plain flour
25 g/1 oz cocoa powder,
    plus extra to decorate
50 ml/2 fl oz cold strong
    black coffee
2 tbsp brandy

topping

600 ml/20 fl oz whipping cream
425 g/15 oz plain chocolate,
    melted and cooled
icing sugar, to decorate

method

1 Grease a 23-cm/9-inch springform cake tin with butter and line the bottom with baking paper. Place the sugar and eggs in a heatproof bowl and set over a pan of hot water. Whisk together until pale and mousse-like. Sift the flour and cocoa powder into a separate bowl, then fold gently into the cake batter. Pour into the prepared tin and bake in a preheated oven, 220°C/425°F/Gas Mark 7, for 7–10 minutes, or until risen and firm to the touch.

2 Transfer to a wire rack to cool. Wash and dry the tin and replace the cooled cake in the tin. Mix the coffee and brandy together and brush over the cake.

3 To make the topping, place the cream in a bowl and whip until very soft peaks form. Carefully fold in the cooled chocolate. Pour the chocolate mixture over the sponge and chill in the refrigerator for 4–5 hours, or until set.

4 To decorate the torte, sift cocoa powder over the top and remove carefully from the tin. Using strips of card or waxed paper as a mask, sift bands of icing sugar over the torte to create a striped pattern. To serve, cut into slices with a hot knife.

moroccan orange & almond cake

ingredients

serves 8

1 orange
115 g/4 oz butter, softened,
    plus extra for greasing
115 g/4 oz golden caster sugar
2 eggs, beaten
175 g/6 oz semolina
100 g/3½ oz ground almonds
1½ tsp baking powder
icing sugar, for dusting
strained plain yogurt, to serve

syrup

300 ml/10 fl oz orange juice
130 g/4¼ oz caster sugar
8 cardamom pods, crushed

method

1 Grate the rind from the orange, reserving some for the decoration, and squeeze the juice from one half. Place the butter, orange rind and sugar in a bowl and beat together until light and fluffy. Beat in the eggs.

2 In a separate bowl, mix the semolina, ground almonds and baking powder, then fold into the creamed mixture with the orange juice. Spoon the batter into a greased and base-lined 20-cm/8-inch cake tin and bake in a preheated oven, 180°C/350°F/Gas Mark 4, for 30–40 minutes, or until well risen and a skewer inserted into the centre comes out clean. Cool in the tin for 10 minutes.

3 To make the syrup, place the orange juice, sugar and cardamom pods in a pan over low heat and stir until the sugar has dissolved. Bring to a boil and simmer for 4 minutes, or until syrupy.

4 Turn the cake out into a deep serving dish. Using a skewer, make holes over the surface of the warm cake. Strain the syrup into a separate bowl and spoon three-quarters of it over the cake, then set aside for 30 minutes. Dust the cake with icing sugar and cut into slices. Serve with the remaining syrup drizzled around, accompanied by strained plain yogurt decorated with the reserved orange rind.

caribbean coconut cake

ingredients

serves 8

280 g/10 oz butter, softened,
    plus extra for greasing
175 g/6 oz golden caster sugar
3 eggs
175 g/6 oz self-raising flour
1½ tsp baking powder
½ tsp freshly grated nutmeg
55 g/2 oz dry unsweetened
    coconut
5 tbsp coconut cream
280 g/10 oz icing sugar
5 tbsp pineapple jam
dry unsweetened coconut,
    toasted, to decorate

method

1 Grease and base-line 2 x 20-cm/8-inch sponge cake tins. Place 175 g/6 oz of the butter in a bowl with the sugar and eggs and sift in the flour, baking powder and nutmeg. Beat together until smooth, then stir the coconut and 2 tablespoons of the coconut cream into the mixture.

2 Divide the mixture between the prepared tins and smooth the surface. Bake in a preheated oven, 180°C/350°F/Gas Mark 4, for 25 minutes, or until golden and firm to the touch. Cool in the tins for 5 minutes, then turn out onto a wire rack, peel off the lining paper and cool completely.

3 Sift the icing sugar into a bowl and add the remaining butter and coconut cream. Beat together until smooth. Spread the pineapple jam on one of the cakes and top with just under half of the buttercream. Place the other cake on top. Spread the remaining buttercream on top of the cake and scatter with the toasted coconut.

honey spiced cake

ingredients

serves 8

150 g/5½ oz butter, plus extra
    for greasing
115 g/4 oz brown sugar
175 g/6 oz honey
1 tbsp water
200 g/7 oz self-raising flour
½ tsp ground ginger
½ tsp ground cinnamon
½ tsp caraway seeds
seeds from 8 cardamom pods,
    ground
2 eggs, beaten
350 g/12 oz icing sugar

method

1 Grease an 1-litre/1¾-pint fluted cake tin. Place the
   butter, sugar, honey and water into a heavy-based pan.
   Set over low heat and stir until the butter has melted
   and the sugar has dissolved. Remove from the heat and
   cool for 10 minutes.

2 Sift the flour into a bowl and mix in the ginger,
   cinnamon, caraway seeds and cardamom. Make a well
   in the centre. Pour in the honey mixture and the eggs
   and beat well until smooth. Pour the batter into the
   prepared tin and bake in a preheated oven, 180°C/
   350°F/Gas Mark 4, for 40–50 minutes, or until well risen
   and a skewer inserted into the centre comes out clean.
   Cool in the tin for 5 minutes, then transfer to a wire rack
   to cool completely.

3 Sift the icing sugar into a bowl. Stir in enough warm
   water to make a smooth, flowing icing. Spoon over
   the cake, allowing it to flow down the sides, then
   allow to set.

rich fruit cake

ingredients

serves 4

butter, for greasing
175 g/6 oz pitted unsweetened
    dates
125 g/4½ oz no-soak dried prunes
200 ml/7 fl oz unsweetened
    orange juice
2 tbsp molasses
1 tsp finely grated lemon rind
1 tsp finely grated orange rind
225 g/8 oz wholemeal
    self-raising flour
1 tsp mixed spice
125 g/4½ oz seedless raisins
125 g/4½ oz sultanas
125 g/4½ oz currants
125 g/4½ oz dried cranberries
3 large eggs, separated
1 tbsp apricot jam, warmed

icing

125 g/4½ oz icing sugar
1–2 tsp water
1 tsp vanilla extract
orange and lemon rind strips,
    to decorate

method

1 Grease and line a deep 20-cm/8-inch round cake tin.
Chop the dates and prunes and place in a pan.
Pour over the orange juice and simmer for 10 minutes.
Remove the pan from the heat and beat the fruit
mixture until puréed. Add the molasses and citrus
rinds and cool.

2 Sift the flour and spice into a bowl, adding any bran
that remains in the sieve. Add the dried fruits. When
the date and prune mixture is cool, whisk in the egg
yolks. Whisk the egg whites in a separate, clean bowl
until stiff. Spoon the fruit mixture into the dry
ingredients and mix together.

3 Gently fold in the egg whites. Transfer to the prepared
tin and bake in a preheated oven, 160°C/325°F/Gas
Mark 3, for 1½ hours. Cool in the tin.

4 Remove the cake from the tin and brush the top with
jam. To make the icing, sift the sugar into a bowl and
mix with enough water and the vanilla extract to form
a soft icing. Lay the icing over the top of the cake and
trim the edges. Decorate with orange and lemon rind.

chocolate cherry layer cake

ingredients

serves 8

3 tbsp unsalted butter, melted,
    plus extra for greasing
900 g/2 lb fresh cherries, pitted
    and halved
100 ml/3½ fl oz cherry brandy
250 g/9 oz caster sugar
100 g/3½ oz plain flour
50 g/1¼ oz cocoa powder
½ tsp baking powder
4 eggs
1 litre/1¼ pints double cream
grated plain chocolate
whole fresh cherries,
    to decorate

method

1 Grease and line a 23-cm/9-inch springform cake tin. Put the halved cherries into a pan and add the cherry brandy and 3 tablespoons of the sugar. Simmer for 5 minutes. Strain, reserving the syrup. In another bowl, sift together the flour, cocoa and baking powder.

2 Put the eggs in a heatproof bowl and beat in 160 g/5¾ oz of the sugar. Place the bowl over a pan of simmering water and beat for 6 minutes until thickened. Remove from the heat, then gradually fold in the flour mixture and melted butter. Spoon into the cake tin. Bake in a preheated oven, 180°C/350°F/Gas Mark 4, for 40 minutes. Remove from the oven and cool.

3 Turn out the cake and cut in half horizontally. Whip the cream with the remaining sugar. Spread the reserved syrup over the cut sides of the cake. Arrange the cherries over one half, top with a layer of cream and place the other half on top. Cover with cream, press grated chocolate all over and decorate with cherries.

small
bites

iced peanut butter cupcakes

ingredients
serves 16

4 tbsp butter, softened,
　　or soft margarine
225 g/8 oz brown sugar
115 g/4 oz crunchy
　　peanut butter
2 eggs, lightly beaten
1 tsp vanilla extract
225 g/8 oz plain flour
2 tsp baking powder
100 ml/3½ fl oz milk

icing
200 g/7 oz full-fat soft
　　cream cheese
2 tbsp butter, softened
225 g/8 oz icing sugar

method

1 Put 16 muffin paper cases in a muffin tin.

2 Put the butter, sugar and peanut butter in a bowl and beat together for 1–2 minutes, or until well mixed. Gradually add the eggs, beating well after each addition, then add the vanilla extract. Sift in the flour and baking powder and then, using a metal spoon, fold them into the mixture, alternating with the milk. Spoon the batter into the paper cases.

3 Bake the cupcakes in a preheated oven, 180°C/350°F/Gas Mark 4, for 25 minutes, or until well risen and golden brown. Transfer to a wire rack to cool.

4 To make the icing, put the cream cheese and butter in a large bowl and, using an electric hand whisk, beat together until smooth. Sift the icing sugar into the mixture, then beat together until well mixed.

5 When the cupcakes are cold, spread the icing on top of each cupcake, swirling it with a round-bladed knife. Store the cupcakes in the refrigerator until ready to serve.

drizzled honey cupcakes

ingredients

serves 12

85 g/3 oz self-raising flour
¼ tsp ground cinnamon
pinch of ground cloves
pinch of grated nutmeg
6 tbsp butter, softened
85 g/3 oz caster sugar
1 tbsp honey
finely grated rind of 1 orange
2 eggs, lightly beaten
40 g/1½ oz walnut pieces,
    chopped

topping

15 g/½ oz walnut pieces, chopped
¼ tsp ground cinnamon
2 tbsp honey
juice of 1 orange

method

1 Put 12 paper baking cases in a muffin tin, or place
   12 double-layer paper cases on a baking sheet.

2 Sift the flour, cinnamon, cloves and nutmeg together
   into a bowl. Put the butter and sugar in a separate bowl
   and beat together until light and fluffy. Beat in the
   honey and orange rind, then gradually add the eggs,
   beating well after each addition. Using a metal spoon,
   fold in the flour mixture. Stir in the walnuts, then
   spoon the batter into the paper cases.

3 Bake the cupcakes in a preheated oven, 190°C/375°F/
   Gas Mark 5, for 20 minutes, or until well risen and
   golden brown. Transfer to a wire rack to cool.

4 To make the topping, mix together the walnuts and
   cinnamon. Put the honey and orange juice in a pan
   and heat gently, stirring, until combined.

5 When the cupcakes have almost cooled, prick the tops
   all over with a fork or skewer and then drizzle with the
   warm honey mixture. Sprinkle the walnut mixture over
   the top of each cupcake and serve warm or cold.

sticky gingerbread cupcakes

ingredients

serves 16

115 g/4 oz plain flour
2 tsp ground ginger
¾ tsp ground cinnamon
1 piece of preserved ginger,
    finely chopped
¾ tsp baking soda
4 tbsp milk
6 tbsp butter, softened,
    or soft margarine
70 g/2½ oz brown sugar
2 tbsp molasses
2 eggs, lightly beaten
pieces of preserved ginger,
    to decorate

icing

6 tbsp butter, softened
175 g/6 oz icing sugar
2 tbsp ginger syrup from the
    preserved ginger jar

method

1 Put 16 paper baking cases in a muffin tin, or place
   16 double-layer paper cases on a baking sheet.

2 Sift the flour, ground ginger and cinnamon together
   into a bowl. Add the chopped ginger and toss in the
   flour mixture until well coated. In a separate bowl,
   dissolve the baking soda in the milk.

3 Put the butter and sugar in a bowl and beat together
   until fluffy. Beat in the molasses, then gradually add the
   eggs, beating well after each addition. Beat in the flour
   mixture, then gradually beat in the milk. Spoon the
   batter into the paper cases.

4 Bake the cupcakes in a preheated oven, 160°C/325°F/
   Gas Mark 3, for 20 minutes, or until well risen and
   golden brown. Transfer to a wire rack to cool.

5 To make the icing, put the butter in a bowl and beat
   until fluffy. Sift in the sugar, add the ginger syrup and
   beat together until smooth and creamy. Slice the
   preserved ginger into thin slivers or chop finely.

6 When the cupcakes are cold, spread the icing on top
   of each cupcake, then decorate with pieces of ginger.

banana & pecan cupcakes

ingredients

serves 12

225 g/8 oz plain flour
1¼ tsp baking powder
¼ tsp baking soda
2 ripe bananas
8 tbsp butter, softened,
    or soft margarine
115 g/4 oz caster sugar
½ tsp vanilla extract
2 eggs, lightly beaten
4 tbsp soured cream
55 g/2 oz pecans, coarsely
    chopped

topping
8 tbsp butter, softened
115 g/4 oz icing sugar
25 g/1 oz pecans, chopped

method

1 Line a 12-cup muffin tin with a double layer of muffin paper liners, or place 12 double-layer paper cases on a baking sheet.

2 Sift together the flour, baking powder and baking soda. Peel the bananas, put them in a bowl and mash with a fork.

3 Put the butter, sugar and vanilla in a bowl and beat together until light and fluffy. Gradually add the eggs, beating well after each addition. Stir in the mashed bananas and soured cream. Using a metal spoon, fold in the sifted flour mixture and the chopped nuts, then spoon the batter into the paper cases.

4 Bake the cupcakes in a preheated oven, 190°C/375°F/Gas Mark 5, for 20 minutes, or until well risen and golden brown. Transfer to a wire rack to cool.

5 To make the topping, beat the butter in a bowl until fluffy. Sift in the icing sugar and mix together well. Spread the icing on top of each cupcake and sprinkle with the chopped pecans before serving.

apple & cinnamon muffins

ingredients

serves 6

85 g/3 oz plain
    wholemeal flour
70 g/2½ oz plain flour
1½ tsp baking powder
pinch of salt
1 tsp ground cinnamon
40 g/1½ oz golden caster sugar
2 small eating apples, peeled,
    cored and finely chopped
125 ml/4 fl oz milk
1 egg, beaten
4 tbsp butter, melted

topping

12 brown sugar lumps, coarsely
    crushed
½ tsp ground cinnamon

method

1 Place 6 muffin paper liners in a muffin tin.

2 Sift both flours, baking powder, salt and cinnamon together into a large bowl and stir in the sugar and chopped apples. Place the milk, egg and butter in a separate bowl and mix. Add the wet ingredients to the dry ingredients and gently stir until just combined.

3 Divide the batter evenly between the paper liners. To make the topping, mix the crushed sugar lumps and cinnamon together and sprinkle over the muffins. Bake in a preheated oven, 200°C/400°F/Gas Mark 6, for 20–25 minutes, or until risen and golden.

4 Remove the muffins from the oven and serve warm or place them on a wire rack to cool.

moist walnut cupcakes

ingredients

serves 12

85 g/3 oz walnuts
4 tbsp butter, softened
100 g/3½ oz caster sugar
grated rind of ½ lemon
70 g/2½ oz self-raising flour
2 eggs
12 walnut halves, to decorate

icing

4 tbsp butter, softened
85 g/3 oz icing sugar
grated rind of ½ lemon
1 tsp lemon juice

method

1 Put 12 paper baking cases in a muffin tin, or place 12 double-layer paper cases on a baking sheet.

2 Put the walnuts in a food processor and, using a pulsating action, blend until finely ground, being careful not to overgrind, which will turn them to oil. Add the butter, cut into small pieces, along with the sugar, lemon rind, flour and eggs, then blend until evenly mixed. Spoon the batter into the paper cases.

3 Bake the cupcakes in a preheated oven, 190°C/375°F/ Gas Mark 5, for 20 minutes, or until well risen and golden brown. Transfer to a wire rack to cool.

4 To make the icing, put the butter in a bowl and beat until fluffy. Sift in the icing sugar, add the lemon rind and juice and mix well.

5 When the cupcakes are cold, spread the icing on top of each cupcake and top with a walnut to decorate.

rose petal cupcakes

ingredients

serves 12

8 tbsp butter, softened
115 g/4 oz caster sugar
2 eggs, lightly beaten
1 tbsp milk
few drops of extract of rose oil
¼ tsp vanilla extract
175 g/6 oz self-raising flour

icing

6 tbsp butter, softened
175 g/6 oz icing sugar
pink or purple food colouring
     (optional)
silver dragées (cake decoration
     balls), to decorate

candied rose petals

12–24 rose petals
lightly beaten egg white,
     for brushing
caster sugar, for sprinkling

method

1 To make the candied rose petals, gently rinse the petals and dry well with kitchen paper. Using a pastry brush, paint both sides of a rose petal with egg white, then coat well with caster sugar. Place on a tray and repeat with the remaining petals. Cover the tray with foil and set aside to dry overnight.

2 Put 12 paper baking cases in a muffin tin, or place 12 double-layer paper cases on a baking sheet.

3 Put the butter and sugar in a bowl and beat together until light and fluffy. Gradually add the eggs, beating well after each addition. Stir in the milk, rose oil extract and vanilla extract then, using a metal spoon, fold in the flour. Spoon the batter into the paper cases.

4 Bake the cupcakes in a preheated oven, 200°C/400°F/ Gas Mark 6, for 12–15 minutes until well risen and golden brown. Transfer to a wire rack to cool.

5 To make the icing, put the butter in a large bowl and beat until fluffy. Sift in the icing sugar and mix well together. If wished, add a few drops of pink or purple food colouring to complement the rose petals.

6 When the cupcakes are cold, spread the icing on top of each cake. Top with 1–2 candied rose petals and sprinkle with silver dragées to decorate.

lemon butterfly cakes

ingredients

serves 12

115 g/4 oz self-raising flour
½ tsp baking powder
8 tbsp soft margarine
115 g/4 oz caster sugar
2 eggs, lightly beaten
finely grated rind of ½ lemon
2 tbsp milk
icing sugar, for dusting

lemon filling

6 tbsp butter, softened
175 g/6 oz icing sugar
1 tbsp lemon juice

method

1 Put 12 paper baking cases in a muffin tin, or place 12 double-layer paper cases on a baking sheet.

2 Sift the flour and baking powder into a large bowl. Add the margarine, sugar, eggs, lemon rind and milk and, using an electric hand whisk, beat together until smooth. Spoon the batter into the paper cases.

3 Bake the cupcakes in a preheated oven, 190°C/375°F/ Gas Mark 5, for 15–20 minutes, or until well risen and golden brown. Transfer to a wire rack to cool.

4 To make the filling, put the butter in a bowl and beat until fluffy. Sift in the icing sugar, add the lemon juice and beat together until smooth and creamy.

5 When the cupcakes are cold, use a serrated knife to cut a circle from the top of each cupcake and then cut each circle in half. Spread or pipe a little of the buttercream filling into the centre of each cupcake, then press the 2 semicircular halves into it at an angle to resemble butterfly wings. Dust the cakes with sifted icing sugar before serving.

toffee apple cakes

ingredients

serves 12

2 eating apples
1 tbsp lemon juice
250 g/9 oz plain flour
2 tsp baking powder
1½ tsp ground cinnamon
70 g/2½ oz light muscovado sugar
55 g/2 oz butter, plus extra
    for greasing
100 ml/3½ fl oz milk
100 ml/3½ fl oz apple juice
1 egg, beaten

topping

2 tbsp single cream
40 g/1½ oz light muscovado sugar
15 g/½ oz unsalted butter

method

1 Grease a 12-cup muffin tin (preferably non-stick).

2 Core and coarsely grate one of the apples. Slice the remaining apple into 5-mm/¼-inch thick wedges and toss in the lemon juice. Sift together the flour, baking powder and cinnamon, then stir in the sugar and grated apple.

3 Melt the butter and mix with the milk, apple juice and egg. Stir the liquid mixture into the dry ingredients, mixing lightly until just combined.

4 Spoon the mixture into the prepared muffin tin. Arrange two apple slices on top of each.

5 Bake in a preheated oven, 200°C/400°F/Gas Mark 6, for 20–25 minutes or until risen, firm and golden brown. Run a knife round the edge of each bun to loosen, then turn out onto a wire rack to cool.

6 For the topping, place all the ingredients in a small saucepan and heat, stirring, until the sugar has dissolved. Increase the heat and boil rapidly for 2 minutes, or until slightly thickened and syrupy. Cool slightly, then drizzle over the cakes and leave to set.

warm molten-centred chocolate cupcakes

ingredients

serves 8

4 tbsp soft margarine
55 g/2 oz caster sugar
1 large egg
85 g/3 oz self-raising flour
1 tbsp cocoa powder
55 g/2 oz plain chocolate
icing sugar, for dusting

method

1 Put 8 paper baking cases in a muffin tin, or place 8 double-layer paper cases on a baking sheet.

2 Put the margarine, sugar, egg, flour and cocoa in a large bowl and, using an electric hand whisk, beat together until just smooth.

3 Spoon half of the batter into the paper cases. Using a teaspoon, make an indentation in the centre of each cake. Break the chocolate evenly into 8 squares and place a piece in each indentation, then spoon the remaining cake batter on top.

4 Bake the cupcakes in a preheated oven, 190°C/375°F/ Gas Mark 5, for 20 minutes, or until well risen and springy to the touch. Leave the cupcakes for about 2–3 minutes before serving warm, dusted with sifted icing sugar.

low-fat blueberry muffins

ingredients

serves 12

225 g/8 oz plain flour

1 tsp bicarbonate of soda

¼ tsp salt

1 tsp allspice

115 g/4 oz caster sugar

3 large egg whites

3 tbsp low-fat margarine

150 ml/5 fl oz thick low-fat
  natural yogurt or
  blueberry-flavoured yogurt

1 tsp vanilla extract

85 g/3 oz fresh blueberries

method

1 Place 12 paper muffin cases in a muffin tin.

2 Sift the flour, bicarbonate of soda, salt and half the
  allspice into a large mixing bowl. Add 6 tablespoons
  of the sugar and mix together well.

3 In a separate bowl, whisk the egg whites together.
  Add the margarine, yogurt and vanilla extract and
  mix together well, then stir in the blueberries until
  thoroughly mixed. Add the fruit mixture to the dry
  ingredients, then gently stir until just combined.
  Do not overstir the mixture – it is fine for it to be
  a little lumpy.

4 Divide the mixture evenly between the paper cases
  (they should be about two-thirds full). Mix the
  remaining sugar with the remaining allspice, then
  sprinkle the mixture over the muffins.

5 Bake in a preheated oven, 190°C/375°F/Gas Mark 5,
  for 25 minutes, or until risen and golden. Remove the
  muffins from the oven and serve warm, or place them
  on a wire rack to cool completely.

white chocolate brownies

ingredients

serves 9

115 g/4 oz unsalted butter,
    plus extra for greasing
225 g/8 oz white chocolate
115 g/4 oz walnut pieces
2 eggs
115 g/4 oz soft brown sugar
115 g/4 oz self-raising flour

method

1 Lightly grease an 18-cm/7-inch square cake tin
   with butter.

2 Coarsely chop 175 g/6 oz of chocolate and all the
   walnuts. Put the remaining chocolate and the butter
   in a heatproof bowl set over a pan of gently simmering
   water. When melted, stir together, then set aside to
   cool slightly.

3 Whisk the eggs and sugar together, then beat in the
   cooled chocolate mixture until well mixed. Fold in the
   flour, chopped chocolate and the walnuts. Turn the
   mixture into the prepared tin and smooth the surface.

4 Transfer the tin to a preheated oven, 180°C/350°F/Gas
   Mark 4, and bake for 30 minutes, or until just set.
   The mixture should still be a little soft in the centre.
   Remove from the oven and cool in the tin, then cut
   the brownies into 9 squares before serving.

devil's food cakes with chocolate icing

ingredients

serves 18

3 ½ tbsp soft margarine
115 g/4 oz brown sugar
2 large eggs
115 g/4 oz plain flour
½ tsp baking soda
25 g/1 oz cocoa powder
125 ml/4 fl oz soured cream

icing

125 g/4½ oz plain chocolate
2 tbsp caster sugar
150 ml/5 fl oz soured cream

chocolate curls (optional)

100 g/3½ oz plain chocolate

method

1 Put 18 paper baking cases in a muffin tin, or put 18 double-layer paper cases on a baking sheet.

2 Put the margarine, sugar, eggs, flour, baking soda and cocoa in a large bowl and, using an electric hand whisk, beat together until just smooth. Using a metal spoon, fold in the soured cream. Spoon the batter into the paper cases.

3 Bake the cupcakes in a preheated oven, 180°C/350°F/ Gas Mark 4, for 20 minutes, or until well risen and firm to the touch. Transfer to a wire rack to cool.

4 To make the icing, break the chocolate into a heatproof bowl. Set the bowl over a pan of gently simmering water and heat until melted, stirring occasionally.

5 Remove from the heat and cool slightly, then whisk in the sugar and soured cream until combined. Spread the icing over the tops of the cupcakes and allow to set in the refrigerator before serving. If liked, serve decorated with chocolate curls made by shaving plain chocolate with a potato peeler.

fig & almond muffins

ingredients

serves 12

2 tbsp sunflower or peanut oil,
    plus extra for oiling
    (if using)
250 g/9 oz plain flour
1 tsp baking soda
½ tsp salt
225 g/8 oz raw sugar
85 g/3 oz dried figs, chopped
115 g/4 oz almonds, chopped
200 ml/7 fl oz water
1 tsp almond extract
2 tbsp chopped almonds,
    to decorate

method

1 Oil a 12-cup muffin tin with sunflower oil, or line it with
12 muffin paper liners. Sift the flour, baking soda and
salt into a mixing bowl, then add the raw sugar and
stir together.

2 In a separate bowl, mix the figs, almonds and the
remaining sunflower oil together, then stir in the water
and almond extract. Add the fruit and nut mixture to
the flour mixture and gently stir together. Do not
overstir – it is fine for it to be a little lumpy.

3 Divide the muffin batter evenly between the 12 cups
in the muffin tin or the paper liners (they should be
about two-thirds full), then sprinkle over the remaining
chopped almonds to decorate. Transfer to a preheated
oven, 190°C/375°F/Gas Mark 5, and bake for 25 minutes,
or until risen and golden.

4 Remove the muffins from the oven and serve warm,
or place them on a wire rack to cool.

fudge nut muffins

ingredients

serves 12

250 g/9 oz plain flour
4 tsp baking powder
85 g/3 oz caster sugar
6 tbsp crunchy peanut butter
1 large egg, beaten
4 tbsp butter, melted
175 ml/6 fl oz milk
150 g/5½ oz vanilla fudge,
   cut into small pieces
3 tbsp coarsely chopped
   unsalted peanuts

method

1 Line a 12-cup muffin tin with double muffin paper liners. Sift the flour and baking powder into a bowl. Stir in the caster sugar. Add the peanut butter and stir until the mixture resembles breadcrumbs.

2 Place the egg, butter and milk in a separate bowl and beat until blended, then stir into the dry ingredients until just blended. Lightly stir in the fudge pieces. Divide the batter evenly between the muffin liners.

3 Sprinkle the chopped peanuts on top and bake in a preheated oven, 200°C/400°F/Gas Mark 6, for 20–25 minutes until well risen and firm to the touch. Remove the muffins from the oven and cool for 2 minutes, then place them on a wire rack to cool completely.

variation

For a special treat, try a flavoured fudge, such as caramel, mint, banana or even a whiskey-flavoured fudge.

spiced chocolate muffins

ingredients

serves 12

100 g/3½ oz butter, softened
150 g/5 oz caster sugar
115 g/4 oz brown sugar
2 large eggs
150 ml/5 fl oz soured cream
5 tbsp milk
250 g/9 oz plain flour
1 tsp baking soda
2 tbsp cocoa powder
1 tsp allspice
200 g/7 oz plain chocolate chips

method

1 Line a 12-cup muffin tin with muffin liners.

2 Place the butter, caster sugar and brown sugar in a
bowl and beat well. Beat in the eggs, soured cream and
milk until thoroughly mixed. Sift the flour, baking soda,
cocoa and allspice into a separate bowl and stir into
the mixture. Add the chocolate chips and mix well.
Divide the batter evenly between the paper liners.
Bake in a preheated oven, 190°C/375°F/Gas Mark 5,
for 25–30 minutes.

3 Remove from the oven and cool for 10 minutes. Place
them on a wire rack to cool completely. Store in an
airtight container until required.

fruit & nut squares

ingredients

serves 9

115 g/4 oz unsalted butter,
　plus extra for greasing
2 tbsp honey
1 egg, beaten
85 g/3 oz ground almonds
115 g/4 oz no-soak dried apricots,
　finely chopped
55 g/2 oz dried cherries
55 g/2 oz toasted chopped
　hazelnuts
25 g/1 oz sesame seeds
85 g/3 oz rolled oats

method

1 Lightly grease an 18-cm/7-inch shallow, square baking tin with butter. Beat the remaining butter with the honey in a bowl until creamy, then beat in the egg with the almonds.

2 Add the remaining ingredients and mix together. Press into the prepared tin, ensuring that the mixture is firmly packed, and smooth the surface.

3 Bake in a preheated oven, 180°C/350°F/Gas Mark 4, for 20–25 minutes, or until firm to the touch and golden brown.

4 Remove from the oven and let stand for 10 minutes before marking into squares. Cool completely before removing from the tin. Store in an airtight container.

strawberry petits choux

ingredients

serves 12

filling and topping
2 tsp powdered gelatine
2 tbsp water
350 g/12 oz strawberries
225 g/8 oz ricotta cheese
1 tbsp caster sugar
2 tsp crème de fraises de bois
icing sugar, for dusting

petits choux
100 g/3¹/₂ oz plain flour
2 tbsp cocoa powder
pinch of salt
6 tbsp unsalted butter
225 ml/8 fl oz water
2 eggs, plus 1 egg white, beaten

method

1 Sprinkle the gelatine over the water in a heatproof bowl to soften. Place the bowl over a saucepan of simmering water and stir until the gelatine dissolves.

2 Place 225 g/8 oz of the strawberries in a blender with the ricotta, sugar, liqueur and gelatine. Process briefly. Transfer to a bowl, cover and chill for 1–1¹/₂ hours, until set. Line a baking tray with baking paper.

3 To make the petits choux, sift together the flour, cocoa powder and salt. Put the butter and water into a heavy-based saucepan and heat gently until the butter has melted. Remove the saucepan from the heat and add the flour mixture, stirring well. Leave to cool.

4 Gradually beat the eggs and egg white into the flour paste until smooth and glossy. Drop 12 rounded tablespoonfuls of the mixture onto the prepared baking tray and bake in a preheated oven, 220°C/425°F/Gas Mark 7, for 20–25 minutes, until puffed up and crisp. Remove from the oven and make a slit in the side of each petit chou. Return to the oven for 5 minutes. Transfer to a wire rack.

5 Slice the remaining strawberries. Cut the petits choux in half, divide the mousse and strawberry slices between them, then replace the tops. Dust lightly with icing sugar and keep cool before serving.

chocolate chip cookies

ingredients

serves 30

unsalted butter, for greasing
175 g/6 oz plain flour
1 tsp baking powder
125 g/4¹/₂ oz soft margarine
85 g/3 oz light muscovado sugar
55 g/2 oz caster sugar
¹/₂ tsp vanilla extract
1 egg
125 g/4¹/₂ oz plain chocolate chips

method

1 Lightly grease two baking trays.

2 Place all of the ingredients in a large mixing bowl and beat until well combined.

3 Place tablespoonfuls of the mixture onto the prepared baking trays, spacing them well apart to allow for spreading during cooking.

4 Bake in a preheated oven, 190°C/375°F/Gas Mark 5, for 10–12 minutes, or until the cookies are golden brown.

5 Using a palette knife, transfer the cookies to a wire rack to cool completely.

shortbread

ingredients

serves 8

175 g/6 oz plain flour,
    plus extra for dusting
pinch of salt
55 g/2 oz caster sugar,
    plus extra for sprinkling
115 g/4 oz butter, cut into small
    pieces, plus extra for greasing

method

1 Grease a 20-cm/8-inch fluted round tart tin.

2 Mix together the flour, salt and sugar. Rub the butter into the dry ingredients. Continue to work the mixture until it forms a soft dough. Make sure you do not overwork the shortbread or it will be tough, not crumbly as it should be.

3 Lightly press the dough into the prepared tart tin. If you don't have a fluted tin, roll out the dough on a lightly floured board, place on a baking tray and pinch the edges to form a scalloped pattern.

4 Mark into eight pieces with a knife. Prick all over with a fork and bake in a preheated oven, 150°C/300°F/ Gas Mark 2, for 45–50 minutes, until the shortbread is firm and just coloured.

5 Leave to cool in the tin and sprinkle with the sugar. Cut into portions and remove to a wire rack to cool.

variation

For an extra-indulgent version, add 40 g/1½ oz chocolate chips to the shortbread surface just after pressing the dough into the prepared tin (step 3).

lavender biscuits

ingredients

serves 12

55 g/2 oz golden caster sugar
1 tsp chopped lavender leaves
115 g/4 oz butter, softened,
    plus extra for greasing
finely grated rind of 1 lemon
175 g/6 oz plain flour

method

1 Place the sugar and lavender leaves in a food processor. Process until the lavender is very finely chopped, then add the butter and lemon rind and process until light and fluffy. Transfer to a large bowl. Sift in the flour and beat until the mixture forms a stiff dough.

2 Place the dough on a sheet of baking paper and place another sheet on top. Gently press down with a rolling pin and roll out to 3–5 mm/⅛–¼ inch thick. Remove the top sheet of paper and stamp out circles from the dough using a 7-cm/2¾-inch round biscuit cutter. Re-knead and re-roll the dough trimmings and stamp out more biscuits.

3 Using a spatula, carefully transfer the biscuits to a large, greased baking sheet. Prick the biscuits with a fork and bake in a preheated oven, 150°C/300°F/Gas Mark 2, for 12 minutes, or until pale golden brown. Cool on the baking sheet for 2 minutes, then transfer to a wire rack to cool completely.

desserts

apple pie

ingredients

serves 6–8

pastry

175 g/6 oz plain flour

pinch of salt

85 g/3 oz butter or margarine, cut into small pieces

85 g/3 oz lard or white vegetable fat, cut into small pieces

about 1–2 tbsp water

beaten egg or milk, for glazing

filling

750 g–1 kg/1 lb 10 oz–2 lb 4 oz cooking apples, peeled, cored and sliced

125 g/4½ oz soft light brown or caster sugar, plus extra for sprinkling

½–1 tsp ground cinnamon, mixed spice or ground ginger

about 1–2 tbsp water

method

1 To make the pastry, sift the flour and salt into a mixing bowl. Add the butter and lard, and rub in with your fingertips until the mixture resembles fine breadcrumbs. Add enough cold water to mix to a firm dough. Wrap in clingfilm and chill in the refrigerator for 30 minutes.

2 Roll out almost two thirds of the pastry thinly and use to line a deep 23-cm/9-inch pie plate.

3 For the filling, mix the apples with the sugar and spices, and pack into the pastry case – the filling can come up above the rim. Add the water, if needed, particularly if the apples are not very juicy. Roll out the remaining pastry to form a lid. Dampen the edges of the pie rim with water and position the lid, pressing the edges firmly together. Trim and crimp the edges.

4 Use the pastry trimmings to cut out leaves or other shapes to decorate the top of the pie. Glaze the top of the pie with beaten egg or milk, make one or two slits in the top and place the pie on a baking tray.

5 Bake in a preheated oven, 220°C/425°F/Gas Mark 7, for 20 minutes, then reduce the temperature to 180°C/350°F/Gas Mark 4 and bake for a further 30 minutes, or until the pastry is a light golden brown. Serve hot or cold, sprinkled with sugar.

latticed cherry pie

ingredients

serves 8

pastry

140 g/5 oz plain flour, plus extra
    for dusting
¼ tsp baking powder
½ tsp mixed spice
½ tsp salt
50 g/1¾ oz caster sugar
55 g/2 oz cold unsalted butter,
    diced, plus extra for greasing
1 egg, beaten, plus extra
    for glazing

filling

900 g/2 lb stoned fresh cherries,
    or canned cherries, drained
150 g/5 oz caster sugar
½ tsp almond extract
2 tsp cherry brandy
¼ tsp mixed spice
2 tbsp cornflour
2 tbsp water
25 g/1 oz butter

method

1 To make the pastry, sift the flour and baking powder
    into a large bowl. Stir in the mixed spice, salt and sugar.
    Rub in the butter until the mixture resembles fine
    breadcrumbs. Add the beaten egg and mix to a firm
    dough. Cut the dough in half and roll each half into
    a ball. Wrap in clingfilm and chill for 30 minutes.

2 Roll the pastry into two 30-cm/12-inch rounds and use
    one to line the tart tin.

3 To make the filling, put half the cherries and the sugar
    into a large saucepan. Simmer over a low heat, stirring
    until the sugar has melted. Stir in the almond extract,
    brandy and mixed spice. In a separate bowl, mix the
    cornflour and water to form a paste. Remove the
    saucepan from the heat, stir in the cornflour paste.
    Return to the heat and stir constantly until the mixture
    boils and thickens. Leave to cool. Stir in the remaining
    cherries, pour into the pastry case, and dot with butter.

4 Cut the remaining pastry round into long strips about
    1 cm/½ inch wide. Lay the strips to form a lattice. Trim
    off the edges. Crimp around the rim, then brush the
    top with beaten egg. Cover with foil, then bake in
    a preheated oven, 220°C/425°F/Gas Mark 7, for
    30 minutes. Discard the foil, then bake for a further
    15 minutes, or until golden.

forest fruit pie

ingredients

serves 4

filling

225 g/8 oz blueberries

225 g/8 oz raspberries

225 g/8 oz blackberries

100 g/3½ oz caster sugar

2 tbsp icing sugar,
    to decorate

whipped cream, to serve (optional)

pastry

225 g/8 oz plain flour, plus extra
    for dusting

25 g/1 oz ground hazelnuts

100 g/3½ oz butter, cut into small
    pieces, plus extra for greasing

finely grated rind of 1 lemon

1 egg yolk, beaten

4 tbsp milk

method

1 Place the fruit in a pan with 3 tablespoons of the
    caster sugar and simmer gently, stirring frequently,
    for 5 minutes. Remove the pan from the heat.

2 Sift the flour into a bowl, then add the hazelnuts.
    Rub in the butter with the fingertips until the mixture
    resembles breadcrumbs, then sift in the remaining
    sugar. Add the lemon rind, egg yolk and 3 tablespoons
    of the milk and mix. Turn out onto a lightly floured
    work surface and knead briefly. Wrap and chill in the
    refrigerator for 30 minutes.

3 Grease a 20-cm/8-inch pie dish with butter. Roll out
    two-thirds of the pastry to a thickness of 5 mm/¼ inch
    and use it to line the base and side of the dish. Spoon
    the fruit into the pastry case. Brush the rim with water,
    then roll out the remaining pastry to cover the pie. Trim
    and crimp round the edge, then make 2 small slits
    in the top and decorate with 2 leaf shapes cut out from
    the dough trimmings. Brush all over with the remaining
    milk. Bake in a preheated oven, 190°C/375°F/Gas Mark 5,
    for 40 minutes.

4 Remove the pie from the oven, sprinkle with the icing
    sugar and serve with whipped cream, if using.

mississippi mud pie

ingredients

serves 8

pastry

225 g/8 oz plain flour, plus extra
    for dusting
2 tbsp cocoa powder
150 g/5½ oz butter
2 tbsp caster sugar
1–2 tbsp cold water

filling

175 g/6 oz butter
350 g/12 oz brown sugar
4 eggs, lightly beaten
4 tbsp cocoa powder, sifted
150 g/5½ oz plain chocolate
300 ml/10 fl oz single cream
1 tsp chocolate extract

to decorate

425 ml/15 fl oz double
    cream, whipped
chocolate flakes and curls

method

1 To make the pastry, sift the flour and cocoa into a
mixing bowl. Rub in the butter with the fingertips
until the mixture resembles fine breadcrumbs. Stir
in the sugar and enough cold water to mix to a soft
dough. Wrap the dough and chill in the refrigerator
for 15 minutes.

2 Roll out the dough on a lightly floured work surface
and use to line a 23-cm/9-inch loose-based tart tin or
ceramic pie dish. Line with baking paper and fill with
dried beans. Bake in a preheated oven, 190°C/375°F/
Gas Mark 5, for 15 minutes. Remove from the oven and
take out the paper and beans. Bake the pastry case for
a further 10 minutes.

3 To make the filling, beat the butter and sugar together
in a bowl and gradually beat in the eggs with the
cocoa. Melt the chocolate and beat it into the mixture
with the single cream and the chocolate extract.

4 Reduce the temperature of the oven to 160°C/325°F/
Gas Mark 3. Pour the mixture into the pastry case and
bake for 45 minutes, or until the filling has set gently.

5 Cool the mud pie completely, then transfer it to a
serving plate, if you like. Cover with the whipped
cream. Decorate the pie with chocolate flakes and
curls and then chill until ready to serve.

banoffee pie

ingredients

serves 4

filling

3 x 400 g/14 oz cans sweetened
    condensed milk
4 ripe bananas
juice of ½ lemon
1 tsp vanilla extract
75 g/2¾ oz plain chocolate, grated
475 ml/16 fl oz double cream,
    whipped

biscuit base

85 g/3 oz butter, melted,
    plus extra for greasing
150 g/5½ oz digestive biscuits,
    crushed into crumbs
25 g/1 oz shelled almonds,
    toasted and ground
25 g/1 oz shelled hazelnuts,
    toasted and ground

method

1 Place the unopened cans of milk in a large pan and
    add enough water to cover them. Bring to a boil, then
    reduce the heat and simmer for 2 hours, topping up
    the water level to keep the cans covered. Carefully lift
    out the hot cans from the pan and cool.

2 Place the butter in a bowl and add the crushed
    digestive biscuits and ground nuts. Mix together well,
    then press the mixture evenly into the base and side
    of a greased 23-cm/9-inch tart tin. Bake in a preheated
    oven, 180°C/350°F/Gas Mark 4, for 10–12 minutes, then
    remove from the oven and cool.

3 Peel and slice the bananas and place in a bowl.
    Squeeze over the juice from the lemon, add the vanilla
    extract and mix together. Spread the banana mixture
    over the biscuit base in the tin, then spoon over the
    contents of the cooled cans of condensed milk.

4 Sprinkle over 50 g/1¾ oz of the chocolate, then top
    with a layer of whipped cream. Sprinkle over the
    remaining grated chocolate and serve the pie at
    room temperature.

pecan pie

ingredients

serves 8

pastry

250 g/9 oz plain flour
pinch of salt
115 g/4 oz butter, cut into
    small pieces
1 tbsp lard or vegetable
    shortening, cut into
    small pieces
55 g/2 oz golden caster sugar
6 tbsp cold milk

filling

3 eggs
250 g/8 oz muscovado sugar
1 tsp vanilla extract
pinch of salt
85 g/3 oz butter, melted
3 tbsp golden syrup
3 tbsp molasses
350 g/12 oz shelled pecans,
    roughly chopped
pecan halves, to decorate
whipped cream or vanilla ice
    cream, to serve

method

1 To make the pastry, sift the flour and salt into a mixing
   bowl and rub in the butter and lard with the fingertips
   until the mixture resembles fine breadcrumbs. Work in
   the caster sugar and add the milk. Work the mixture
   into a soft dough. Wrap the dough and chill in the
   refrigerator for 30 minutes.

2 Roll out the pastry and use it to line a 23–25-cm/
   9–10-inch tart tin. Trim off the excess by running the
   rolling pin over the top of the tart tin. Line with baking
   paper and fill with dried beans. Bake in a preheated
   oven, 200°C/400°F/Gas Mark 6, for 20 minutes. Take out
   of the oven and remove the paper and dried beans.
   Reduce the oven temperature to 180°C/350°F/
   Gas Mark 4. Place a baking sheet in the oven.

3 To make the filling, place the eggs in a bowl and beat
   lightly. Beat in the muscovado sugar, vanilla extract and
   salt. Stir in the butter, syrup, molasses and chopped
   nuts. Pour into the pastry case and decorate with the
   pecan halves.

4 Place on the heated baking sheet and bake in the oven
   for 35–40 minutes until the filling is set. Serve warm or
   at room temperature with whipped cream or vanilla
   ice cream.

lemon meringue pie

ingredients

serves 8–10

butter, for greasing
plain flour, for dusting
250 g/9 oz ready-made shortcrust
    pastry, thawed if frozen
3 tbsp cornflour
85 g/3 oz caster sugar
grated rind of 3 lemons
300 ml/10 fl oz cold water
150 ml/5 fl oz lemon juice
3 egg yolks
55 g/2 oz unsalted butter,
    cut into small cubes

meringue

3 egg whites
175 g/6 oz caster sugar
1 tsp golden granulated sugar

method

1 Grease a 25-cm/10-inch fluted tart tin. On a lightly floured work surface, roll out the pastry and ease it into the tin, rolling off the excess. Prick the bottom of the tart case and chill, uncovered, for 30 minutes. Line with baking paper and fill with dried beans. Bake on a preheated baking sheet in a preheated oven, 200°C/400°F/Gas Mark 6, for 15 minutes. Remove the beans and paper and return to the oven for 10 minutes. Remove and reduce the temperature to 150°C/300°F/Gas Mark 2.

2 Put the cornflour, sugar and lemon rind into a pan. Blend in a little of the water to make a smooth paste. Gradually add the remaining water and the lemon juice. Bring to a boil over medium heat, stirring continuously. Simmer gently for 1 minute until smooth and glossy. Remove from the heat. Beat in the egg yolks, 1 at a time, then the butter. Place the pan in a bowl of cold water to cool the filling, then spoon it into the tart case.

3 To make the meringue, whisk the egg whites until thick and in soft peaks. Gradually add the caster sugar, whisking well with each addition. Spoon the meringue over the filling to cover it completely. Swirl the meringue into peaks and sprinkle with granulated sugar. Bake for 20–30 minutes until the meringue is crispy and pale gold. Cool slightly before serving.

baked lemon cheesecake

ingredients

serves 6–8

55 g/2 oz butter, plus extra
    for greasing
175 g/6 oz gingernut biscuits,
    crushed
3 lemons
300 g/10½ oz ricotta cheese
200 g/7 oz Greek-style yogurt
4 eggs
1 tbsp cornflour
100 g/3½ oz caster sugar
strips of lemon zest, to decorate
icing sugar, for dusting

method

1 Lightly grease a 20-cm/8-inch round springform cake tin and line the base with non-stick baking paper.

2 Melt the butter and stir in the biscuit crumbs. Press into the base of the prepared cake tin. Chill until firm.

3 Meanwhile, finely grate the rind and squeeze the juice from the lemons. Add the ricotta, yogurt, eggs, cornflour and caster sugar, and whisk until a smooth batter is formed.

4 Carefully pour the mixture into the tin. Bake in a preheated oven, 180°C/350°F/Gas Mark 4, for 40–45 minutes, or until just firm and golden brown.

5 Cool the cheesecake completely in the tin, then run a knife around the edge to loosen and turn out onto a serving plate. Decorate with lemon zest and dust with icing sugar.

new york cheesecake

ingredients

serves 8–10

6 tbsp butter
200 g/7 oz digestive biscuits,
    crushed
sunflower oil, for brushing
400 g/14 oz cream cheese
2 large eggs
140 g/5 oz caster sugar
1½ tsp vanilla extract
450 ml/16 fl oz soured cream

blueberry topping

55 g/2 oz caster sugar
4 tbsp water
250 g/9 oz fresh blueberries
1 tsp arrowroot

method

1 Melt the butter in a pan over low heat. Stir in the crushed biscuits, then spread in a 20-cm/8-inch springform tin brushed with oil. Place the cream cheese, eggs, 100 g/3½ oz of the sugar and ½ teaspoon of the vanilla extract in a food processor and process until smooth. Pour over the biscuit base and smooth the top. Place on a baking sheet and bake in a preheated oven, 190°C/375°F/Gas Mark 5, for 20 minutes until set. Remove from the oven and leave for 20 minutes. Leave the oven on.

2 Mix the cream with the remaining sugar and vanilla extract in a bowl. Spoon over the cheesecake. Return it to the oven for 10 minutes. Remove from the oven, cool, then chill in the refrigerator for 8 hours, or overnight.

3 To make the topping, place the sugar in a pan with 2 tablespoons of the water over low heat and stir until the sugar is dissolved. Increase the heat, add the blueberries, cover and cook until they begin to soften. Remove from the heat. Mix the arrowroot and remaining water in a bowl, add to the fruit and stir until smooth. Return to low heat. Cook until the juice thickens and turns translucent. Set aside to cool.

4 Remove the cheesecake from the tin 1 hour before serving. Spoon the fruit topping over and chill until ready to serve.

raspberry vacherin

ingredients

serves 10

3 egg whites
175 g/6 oz caster sugar
1 tsp cornflour
25 g/1 oz plain chocolate, grated
    filling & topping
175 g/6 oz plain chocolate, broken
    into pieces
450 ml/16 fl oz double cream,
    whipped
280 g/10 oz fresh raspberries
a little melted chocolate,
    to decorate

method

1 Draw three rectangles, measuring 10 x 25 cm/4 x 10 inches, on sheets of baking paper and place on two baking trays.

2 Whisk the egg whites in a mixing bowl until soft peaks form, then gradually whisk in half the sugar and continue whisking until the mixture is very stiff and glossy. Carefully fold in the remaining sugar, cornflour and the grated chocolate with a metal spoon or a palette knife.

3 Spoon the meringue mixture into a piping bag fitted with a 1-cm/½-inch plain nozzle and pipe lines across the rectangles. Bake in a preheated oven, 140°C/275°F/ Gas Mark 1, for 1½ hours, changing the position of the baking trays halfway through. Then turn off the oven and leave the meringues to cool inside the oven.

4 Place the chocolate in a heatproof bowl set over a saucepan of gently simmering water until melted. Spread the chocolate over two of the meringue layers. Leave to harden. Place one chocolate-coated meringue on a plate and top with one third of the cream and raspberries. Place the second chocolate-coated meringue on top and spread with half of the remaining cream and raspberries. Place the last meringue on the top and decorate with the rest of the cream and raspberries. Drizzle the melted chocolate and serve.

strawberry roulade

ingredients

serves 8

3 large eggs
125 g/4½ oz caster sugar
125 g/4½ oz plain flour
1 tbsp hot water
1 tbsp toasted flaked almonds,
    to decorate

filling

200 ml/7 fl oz low-fat
    fromage frais
1 tsp almond extract
225 g/8 oz small strawberries

method

1 Line a 35 x 25-cm/14 x 10-inch Swiss roll tin with baking paper.

2 Place the eggs in a mixing bowl with the caster sugar. Place the bowl over a saucepan of hot, but not boiling, water and whisk until pale and thick.

3 Remove the bowl from the pan. Sift in the flour and fold into the egg mixture with the hot water. Pour the mixture into the prepared tin and bake in a preheated oven, 220°C/425°F/Gas Mark 7, for about 8–10 minutes, until golden and springy to the touch.

4 Remove from the tin and transfer to a sheet of baking paper. Peel off the lining paper and roll up the sponge tightly along with the baking paper. Wrap in a clean tea towel and set aside to cool.

5 For the filling, mix together the fromage frais and almond extract. Cover and chill in the refrigerator until required. Wash, hull and slice the strawberries.

6 Unroll the sponge, spread the fromage frais mixture over it and sprinkle with the sliced strawberries. Roll the sponge up again (without the baking paper this time) and transfer to a serving plate. Sprinkle with the toasted flaked almonds and serve.

pear & pecan strudel

ingredients

serves 4

2 ripe pears
4 tbsp butter
55 g/2 oz fresh white breadcrumbs
55 g/2 oz shelled pecans, chopped
25 g/1 oz muscovado sugar
finely grated rind of 1 orange
100 g/3½ oz filo pastry, thawed
    if frozen
6 tbsp orange blossom honey
2 tbsp orange juice
sifted icing sugar, for dusting
strained plain yogurt, to serve
    (optional)

method

1 Peel, core and chop the pears. Melt 1 tablespoon of the butter in a frying pan and gently sauté the breadcrumbs until golden. Transfer the breadcrumbs to a bowl and add the pears, nuts, muscovado sugar and orange rind. Place the remaining butter in a small pan and heat until melted.

2 Set aside 1 sheet of filo pastry, keeping it well wrapped, and brush the remaining filo sheets with a little melted butter. Spoon a little of the nut filling onto 1 buttered filo sheet, leaving a 2.5-cm/1-inch margin around the edge. Build up the strudel by placing the remaining buttered filo sheets on top of the first, spreading each one with nut filling as you build up the layers. Drizzle the honey and orange juice over the top.

3 Fold the short ends over the filling, then roll up, starting at a long side. Carefully lift onto a baking sheet, with the join uppermost. Brush with any remaining melted butter and crumple the reserved sheet of filo pastry around the strudel. Bake in a preheated oven, 200°C/400°F/Gas Mark 6, for 25 minutes, or until golden and crisp. Dust with sifted icing sugar and serve warm with strained plain yogurt, if using.

peach cobbler

ingredients

serves 4–6

filling

6 peaches, peeled and sliced
4 tbsp caster sugar
½ tbsp lemon juice
1½ tsp cornflour
½ tsp almond or vanilla extract
vanilla or pecan ice cream,
    to serve

topping

175 g/6 oz plain flour
115 g/4 oz caster sugar
1½ tsp baking powder
½ tsp salt
85 g/3 oz butter, diced
1 egg
5–6 tbsp milk

method

1 Place the peaches in a 23-cm/9-inch square ovenproof dish that is also suitable for serving. Add the sugar, lemon juice, cornflour and almond extract and toss together. Bake the peaches in a preheated oven, 220°C/425°F/Gas Mark 7, for 20 minutes.

2 Meanwhile, to make the topping, sift the flour, all but 2 tablespoons of the sugar, the baking powder and salt into a bowl. Rub in the butter with the fingertips until the mixture resembles breadcrumbs. Mix the egg and 5 tablespoons of the milk in a jug, then mix into the dry ingredients with a fork until a soft, sticky dough forms. If the dough seems too dry, stir in the extra tablespoon of milk.

3 Reduce the temperature of the oven to 200°C/400°F/Gas Mark 6. Remove the peaches from the oven and drop spoonfuls of the topping over the surface, without smoothing. Sprinkle with the remaining sugar, return to the oven and bake for a further 15 minutes, or until the topping is golden brown and firm – the topping will spread as it cooks. Serve hot or at room temperature with ice cream.

almond tart

ingredients

serves 8

pastry

280 g/10 oz plain flour, plus extra
    for dusting
150 g/5½ oz caster sugar
1 tsp finely grated lemon rind
pinch of salt
150 g/5½ oz unsalted butter,
    chilled and cut into
    small dice
1 medium egg, beaten lightly
1 tbsp chilled water

filling

175 g/6 oz unsalted butter,
    at room temperature
175 g/6 oz caster sugar
3 large eggs
175 g/6 oz finely
    ground almonds
2 tsp plain flour
1 tbsp finely grated orange rind
½ tsp almond extract
icing sugar, to decorate
soured cream (optional),
    to serve

method

1 To make the pastry, put the flour, sugar, lemon rind and salt in a bowl. Rub or cut in the butter until the mixture resembles fine breadcrumbs. Combine the egg and water, then slowly pour into the flour, stirring with a fork until a coarse mass forms. Shape into a ball and chill for at least 1 hour.

2 Roll out the pastry on a lightly floured work surface until 3 mm/⅛ inch thick. Use to line a greased 25-cm/10-inch tart tin. Return to the refrigerator for 15 minutes, then cover the pastry case with foil and fill with dried beans. Place in a preheated oven, 220°C/425°F/Gas Mark 7, and bake for 12 minutes. Remove the dried beans and foil and return the pastry case to the oven for 4 minutes. Remove from the oven and reduce the oven temperature to 200°C/400°F/Gas Mark 6.

3 Meanwhile, make the filling. Beat the butter and sugar until creamy. Beat in the eggs, 1 at a time. Add the almonds, flour, orange rind and almond extract and beat until blended.

4 Spoon the filling into the pastry case and smooth the surface. Bake for 30–35 minutes until the top is golden and the filling is fully baked. Cool completely on a wire rack, then dust with sifted icing sugar. Serve with a spoonful of soured cream, if using.

pear tarte tatin

ingredients

serves 6

6 tbsp butter
115 g/4 oz caster sugar
6 pears, peeled, halved
    and cored
flour, for dusting
225 g/8 oz ready-made
    puff pastry
double cream, to serve
    (optional)

method

1 Melt the butter and sugar in an ovenproof frying pan over medium heat. Stir carefully for 5 minutes until it turns to a light caramel colour. Take care because it gets very hot.

2 Remove the pan from the heat, place on a heatproof surface and arrange the pears, cut side up, in the caramel. Place one half in the centre and surround it with the others.

3 On a lightly floured work surface, roll out the dough to a round, slightly larger than the frying pan, and place it on top of the pears. Tuck the edges down into the pan.

4 Bake near the top of a preheated oven, 200°C/400°F/ Gas Mark 6, for 20–25 minutes until the pastry is well risen and golden brown. Remove from the oven and cool for 2 minutes.

5 Invert the tart onto a serving dish that is larger than the frying pan and has enough depth to take any juices that may run out. Remember that this is very hot so use a pair of thick oven gloves. Serve warm, with double cream if using.

chocolate fudge tart

ingredients

serves 6

flour, for sprinkling
350 g/12 oz ready-made
    shortcrust pastry
icing sugar, for dusting

filling

140 g/5 oz plain chocolate,
    finely chopped
175 g/6 oz butter, diced
350 g/12 oz golden
    granulated sugar
100 g/3½ oz plain flour
½ tsp vanilla extract
6 eggs, beaten

to decorate

150 ml/5 fl oz whipped cream
ground cinnamon

method

1 Roll out the pastry on a lightly floured work surface and
   use to line a 20-cm/8-inch deep loose-based tart tin.
   Prick the dough base lightly with a fork, then line with
   foil and fill with dried beans. Bake in a preheated oven,
   200°C/400°F/Gas Mark 6, for 12–15 minutes, or until the
   dough no longer looks raw. Remove the beans and foil
   and bake for a further 10 minutes, or until the dough is
   firm. Set aside to cool. Reduce the oven temperature to
   180°C/350°F/Gas Mark 4.

2 To make the filling, place the chocolate and butter in a
   heatproof bowl and set over a pan of gently simmering
   water until melted. Stir until smooth, then remove from
   the heat and cool. Place the sugar, flour, vanilla extract
   and eggs in a separate bowl and whisk until well
   blended. Stir in the butter and chocolate mixture.

3 Pour the filling into the pastry case and bake in the
   oven for 50 minutes, or until the filling is just set.
   Transfer to a wire rack to cool completely. Dust with
   icing sugar before serving with whipped cream
   sprinkled lightly with cinnamon.

toffee apple tart

ingredients

serves 6

butter, for greasing
flour, for sprinkling
300 g/10 oz ready-made
    shortcrust pastry

filling

1.3 kg/3 lb Pippin or other
    firm, sweet apples, peeled
    and cored
1 tsp lemon juice
3 heaped tbsp butter
100 g/3½ oz caster sugar
200 g/7 oz granulated sugar
75 ml/2½ fl oz cold water
150 ml/5 fl oz double cream,
    plus extra for serving

method

1 Lightly grease a 22-cm/9-inch loose-based fluted tart tin.
Roll out the pastry on a lightly floured work surface and
line the tin with it, then roll the rolling pin over the tin to
trim the excess dough. Fit a piece of baking paper into
the tart case and fill with dried beans. Chill in the
refrigerator for 30 minutes, then bake for 10 minutes in
a preheated oven, 190°C/375°F/Gas Mark 5. Remove the
beans and paper and return to the oven for 5 minutes.

2 Meanwhile, take 4 apples, cut each one into 8 pieces
and toss in the lemon juice. Melt the butter in a frying
pan and sauté the apple pieces until just starting to
caramelize and brown on the edges. Remove from the
pan and set aside to cool.

3 Slice the remaining apples thinly, put them in a pan
with the caster sugar and cook for about 20 minutes,
until soft. Spoon into the pastry case and arrange the
reserved apple pieces on top in a circle. Bake for
30 minutes.

4 Put the granulated sugar and water in a pan and
heat until the sugar dissolves. Boil to form a caramel.
Remove from the heat and add the cream, stirring
constantly to combine into toffee. Remove the tart
from the oven, pour the toffee over the apples and
chill for 1 hour. Serve with double cream.

baking
with yeast

crusty white bread

ingredients

makes 1 medium loaf

1 egg
1 egg yolk
hand-hot water, as required
500 g/1 lb 2 oz white bread flour,
    plus extra for dusting
1½ tsp salt
2 tsp sugar
1 tsp easy-blend dried yeast
2 tbsp butter, diced
vegetable oil, for brushing

method

1 Place the egg and egg yolk in a jug and beat lightly to mix. Add enough hand-hot water to make up to 300 ml/10 fl oz. Stir well.

2 Place the flour, salt, sugar and yeast in a large bowl. Add the butter and rub it in with your fingertips until the mixture resembles breadcrumbs. Make a well in the centre, add the egg mixture and work to a smooth dough.

3 Turn the dough out onto a lightly floured work surface and knead for 10 minutes, or until the dough is smooth and elastic. Place the dough in an oiled bowl, cover with clingfilm and leave in a warm place to rise for 1 hour, or until it has doubled in size.

4 Oil a 900-g/2-lb loaf tin. Turn the dough out onto a lightly floured work surface and knead for 1 minute until smooth. Shape the dough the length of the tin and three times the width. Fold the dough into three lengthways and place it in the tin with the join underneath. Cover and leave in a warm place for 30 minutes until it has risen above the tin.

5 Bake in a preheated oven, 220°C/425°F/Gas Mark 7, for 30 minutes, or until firm and golden brown. Test that the loaf is cooked by tapping it on the bottom – it should sound hollow. Transfer to a wire rack to cool completely.

rye bread

ingredients

makes 1 large loaf

450 g/1 lb rye flour

225 g/8 oz strong white flour,
    plus extra for dusting

2 tsp salt

2 tsp soft light brown sugar

1½ tsp easy-blend dried yeast

425 ml/15 fl oz lukewarm water

2 tsp vegetable oil, plus extra
    for brushing

1 egg white

method

1 Sift the flours and salt together into a bowl. Add the sugar and yeast and stir to mix. Make a well in the centre and pour in the lukewarm water and oil. Stir until the dough begins to come together, then knead with your hands until it leaves the side of the bowl. Turn out and knead for 10 minutes, until elastic and smooth.

2 Brush a bowl with oil. Shape the dough into a ball, put it in the bowl and cover with a damp tea towel. Leave to rise in a warm place for 2 hours, until the dough has doubled in volume. Brush a baking tray with oil. Turn out the dough onto a lightly floured surface and knock back with your fist, then knead for a further 10 minutes. Shape the dough into a ball, put it on the prepared baking tray and cover with a damp tea towel. Leave to rise in a warm place for a further 40 minutes, until the dough has doubled in volume.

3 Beat the egg white with 1 tablespoon of water in a bowl. Bake the loaf in a preheated oven, 190°C/375°F/Gas Mark 5, for 20 minutes, then remove from the oven and brush the top with the egg white glaze. Return to the oven and bake for a further 20 minutes. Brush the top of the loaf with the glaze again and return to the oven for 20–30 minutes, until the crust is a rich brown colour and the loaf sounds hollow when tapped on the base with your knuckles. Transfer to a wire rack to cool.

plaited poppy seed bread

ingredients

makes 1 loaf

225 g/8 oz strong white flour,
   plus extra for dusting
1 tsp salt
2 tbsp skimmed milk powder
1½ tbsp caster sugar
1 tsp easy-blend dried yeast
175 ml/6 fl oz lukewarm water
2 tbsp vegetable oil, plus extra
   for brushing
5 tbsp poppy seeds

topping

1 egg yolk
1 tbsp milk
1 tbsp caster sugar
2 tbsp poppy seeds

method

1 Sift the flour and salt together into a bowl and stir in
   the milk powder, sugar and yeast. Make a well in the
   centre and pour in the lukewarm water and oil. Stir
   well. Add the poppy seeds and knead with your hands
   so the dough leaves the side of the bowl. Turn out
   onto a lightly floured surface and knead well for about
   10 minutes, until smooth and elastic.

2 Brush a bowl with oil. Shape the dough into a ball, put
   it in the bowl and cover with a damp tea towel. Leave
   to rise in a warm place for 1 hour, until the dough has
   doubled in volume. Brush a baking tray with oil. Turn
   out the dough, knock back and knead for 1–2 minutes.
   Divide the dough into three equal pieces and shape
   each into a rope 25–30 cm/10–12 inches long.

3 Place the ropes side by side and press them together
   at one end. Plait the dough. Put the loaf on the
   prepared baking tray. Cover with a damp tea towel
   and leave to rise in a warm place for 30 minutes.

4 To make the topping, beat the egg yolk with the
   milk and sugar. Brush the egg glaze over the top and
   sprinkle with the poppy seeds. Bake in a preheated
   oven, 200°C/400°F/Gas Mark 6, for 30–35 minutes, until
   golden brown and the loaf sounds hollow when
   tapped. Transfer to a wire rack to cool.

mixed seed bread

ingredients

makes 1 medium loaf

375 g/13 oz white bread flour,
    plus extra for dusting
125 g/4½ oz rye flour
1½ tbsp skimmed milk powder
1½ tsp salt
1 tbsp brown sugar
1 tsp easy-blend dried yeast
1½ tbsp sunflower oil
2 tsp lemon juice
300 ml/10 fl oz lukewarm water
1 tsp caraway seeds
½ tsp poppy seeds
½ tsp sesame seeds
vegetable oil, for brushing

topping

1 egg white
1 tbsp water
1 tbsp sunflower or
    pumpkin seeds

method

1 Place the flours, milk powder, salt, sugar and yeast in a large bowl. Pour in the oil and add the lemon juice and water. Stir in the seeds and mix well to make a smooth dough.

2 Turn the dough out onto a lightly floured work surface and knead for 10 minutes, or until the dough is smooth and elastic. Place the dough in an oiled bowl, cover with clingfilm and let stand in a warm place to rise for 1 hour, or until it has doubled in size.

3 Oil a 900-g/2-lb loaf tin. Turn the dough out onto a lightly floured work surface and knead for 1 minute until smooth. Shape the dough the length of the tin and three times the width. Fold the dough into three lengthways and place it in the tin with the join underneath. Cover and let stand in a warm place for 30 minutes until it has risen above the tin.

4 For the topping, lightly beat the egg white with the water to make a glaze. Just before baking, brush the glaze over the loaf, then gently press the sunflower or pumpkin seeds all over the top.

5 Bake in a preheated oven, 220°C/425°F/Gas Mark 7, for 30 minutes, or until firm and golden brown. Test that the loaf is cooked by tapping it on the bottom – it should sound hollow. Transfer to a wire rack to cool completely before serving.

fresh croissants

ingredients

serves 12

500 g/1 lb 2 oz white bread flour,
plus extra for dusting
40 g/1½ oz caster sugar
1 tsp salt
2 tsp easy-blend dried yeast
300 ml/10 fl oz milk, heated until
just warm to the touch
300 g/10½ oz butter, softened,
flattened with
a rolling pin between
2 sheets of waxed paper
to form a rectangle
5 mm/¼ inch thick, then
chilled in the refrigerator,
plus extra for greasing
1 egg, lightly beaten with
1 tbsp milk, to glaze
jam, to serve (optional)

you will need

a cardboard triangular template,
base 18 cm/7 inches and sides
20 cm/8 inches

method

1 Stir the dry ingredients in a large bowl. Make a well
in the centre and add the milk. Mix to a soft dough.
Knead on a lightly floured work surface for 5–10
minutes, or until smooth and elastic. Let rise in a large,
greased bowl, covered, in a warm place.

2 Knead the dough for 1 minute. Let the butter soften
slightly. Roll out the dough on a well-floured work
surface to 46 x 15 cm/18 x 6 inches. Place the butter
in the centre. Then with the short end of the dough
towards you, fold the top third down towards the
centre, then fold the bottom third up and squeeze the
edges together gently. Rotate so that the fold is to your
left and the top flap towards your right. Roll out to a
rectangle and fold again. If the butter feels soft, wrap
the dough in clingfilm and chill. Repeat the rolling
process twice more. Cut the dough in half. Roll out one
half into a triangle 5 mm/¼ inch thick (keep the other
half refrigerated). Use the cardboard template to cut
out the croissants.

3 Brush the triangles lightly with the glaze. Roll into
croissant shapes, starting at the base and tucking
under the point. Brush again with the glaze and place
on an ungreased baking sheet. Let double in size, then
bake in a preheated oven, 200°C/400°F/Gas Mark 6, for
15–20 minutes until golden. Serve with jam, if liked.

pains au chocolat

ingredients

serves 8

100 g/3½ oz butter, plus extra
    for greasing
250 g/9 oz white bread flour,
    plus extra for dusting
1 tsp salt
2 tsp easy-blend dried yeast
175 ml/6 fl oz milk
2 tbsp golden caster sugar
1 tbsp oil, plus extra for brushing
115 g/4 oz plain chocolate,
    coarsely chopped

glaze

1 egg yolk
2 tbsp milk

method

1 Grease a baking sheet. Sift the flour and salt into a bowl
    and stir in the yeast. Make a well in the centre. Heat the
    milk in a pan until tepid. Add the sugar and oil and stir
    until the sugar has dissolved. Stir into the flour and mix
    well. Turn the dough out onto a lightly floured work
    surface and knead until smooth, then place in an oiled
    bowl. Cover and let rise in a warm place for 2–3 hours,
    or until doubled in size.

2 Knead on a floured work surface and roll into a
    rectangle 3 times as long as it is wide. Divide the butter
    into thirds. Dot one portion over the top two-thirds of
    the dough, leaving a 1-cm/½-inch margin round the
    edges. Fold the lower third up and the top third down.
    Seal the edges. Give the dough a half-turn. Roll into a
    rectangle. Repeat the process twice, then fold in half.
    Put into an oiled plastic bag. Chill for 1 hour.

3 Cut the dough in half and roll out into 2 rectangles
    of 30 x 15 cm/12 x 6 inches. Cut each half into
    4 rectangles of 15 x 7.5 cm/6 x 3 inches. Sprinkle
    chocolate along one short end of each and roll up.
    Place on the baking sheet in a warm place for 2–3
    hours, or until doubled in size. To glaze, mix the egg
    yolk and milk and brush over the rolls. Bake in a
    preheated oven, 220°C/425°F/Gas Mark 7, for
    15–20 minutes, or until golden and well risen.

stollen

ingredients

serves 10

85 g/3 oz currants
55 g/2 oz raisins
2 tbsp chopped candied peel
55 g/2 oz candied cherries, rinsed,
    dried and quartered
2 tbsp rum
55 g/2 oz butter
175 ml/6 fl oz milk
2 tbsp golden caster sugar
375 g/13 oz strong white bread
    flour, plus extra for dusting
1/2 tsp ground nutmeg
1/2 tsp ground cinnamon
seeds from 3 cardamoms
2 tsp easy-blend dried yeast
finely grated rind of 1 lemon
1 egg, beaten
40 g/1 1/2 oz flaked almonds
vegetable oil, for brushing
175 g/6 oz marzipan
melted butter, for brushing
sifted icing sugar, for dredging

method

1 Place the currants, raisins, peel and cherries in a bowl, stir in the rum and set aside. Place the butter, milk and sugar in a pan over low heat and stir until the sugar dissolves and the butter melts. Cool until lukewarm. Sift the flour, nutmeg and cinnamon into a bowl. Crush the cardamom seeds and add them. Stir in the yeast. Make a well in the centre, stir in the milk mixture, lemon rind and egg and beat into a dough.

2 Turn the dough out onto a floured work surface and knead for 5 minutes. Knead in the soaked fruit and the almonds. Transfer to a clean, oiled bowl. Cover with clingfilm and let stand in a warm place for up to 3 hours, or until doubled in size. Turn out onto a floured work surface, knead for 1–2 minutes, then roll out to a 25-cm/10-inch square.

3 Roll the marzipan into a sausage shorter than the length of the dough. Place in the centre. Fold the dough over the marzipan, overlapping it. Seal the ends. Place seam-side down on a greased baking sheet, cover with oiled clingfilm and let stand in a warm place for up to 2 hours, or until doubled in size. Bake in a preheated oven, 190°C/375°F/Gas Mark 5, for 40 minutes, or until golden and hollow sounding when tapped. Brush with melted butter, dredge with icing sugar and cool on a wire rack.

apricot & walnut bread

ingredients

serves 12

55 g/2 oz butter, plus extra
    for greasing
350 g/12 oz strong white bread
    flour, plus extra
    for dusting
1/2 tsp salt
1 tsp golden caster sugar
2 tsp easy-blend dried yeast
115 g/4 oz no-soak dried apricots,
    chopped
55 g/2 oz chopped walnuts
150 ml/5 fl oz tepid milk
75 ml/2 1/2 fl oz tepid water
1 egg, beaten
vegetable oil, for brushing

topping

85 g/3 oz icing sugar
walnut halves

method

1 Grease and flour a baking sheet. Sift the flour and salt into a warmed bowl and stir in the sugar and yeast. Rub in the butter and add the chopped apricots and walnuts. Make a well in the centre. In a separate bowl, mix together the milk, water and egg. Pour into the dry ingredients and mix to a soft dough. Turn out onto a floured work surface and knead for 10 minutes, or until smooth. Place the dough in a clean bowl brushed with oil, cover with oiled clingfilm and let stand in a warm place for 2–3 hours, or until doubled in size.

2 Turn the dough out onto a floured work surface and knead lightly for 1 minute. Divide into 5 equal pieces and roll each piece into a rope 30 cm/12 inches long. Braid 3 ropes together, pinching the ends to seal, and place on the prepared baking sheet. Twist the remaining 2 ropes together and place on top. Cover lightly with oiled clingfilm and let stand in a warm place for 1–2 hours, or until doubled in size.

3 Bake the bread in a preheated oven, 220°C/425°F/Gas Mark 7, for 10 minutes, then reduce the heat to 190°C/375°F/Gas Mark 5 and bake for a further 20 minutes. Transfer to a wire rack to cool. To make the topping, sift the icing sugar into a bowl, stir in enough water to make a thin icing and drizzle over the loaf. Decorate with walnut halves and serve.

orange & raisin brioches

ingredients

serves 12

55 g/2 oz butter, melted, plus
    extra for greasing
225 g/8 oz strong white bread
    flour, plus extra for dusting
½ tsp salt
2 tsp easy-blend dried yeast
1 tbsp golden caster sugar
55 g/2 oz raisins
grated rind of 1 orange
2 tbsp tepid water
2 eggs, beaten
vegetable oil, for brushing
1 beaten egg, for glazing
butter, to serve (optional)

method

1 Grease 12 individual brioche moulds. Sift the flour and
salt into a warmed bowl and stir in the yeast, sugar,
raisins and orange rind. Make a well in the centre. In a
separate bowl, mix together the water, eggs and melted
butter and pour into the dry ingredients. Beat vigorously
to make a soft dough. Turn out onto a lightly floured
work surface and knead for 5 minutes, or until smooth
and elastic. Brush a clean bowl with oil. Place the dough
in the bowl, cover with clingfilm and let stand in a warm
place for 1 hour, or until doubled in size.

2 Turn out onto a floured work surface, knead lightly for
1 minute, then roll into a rope shape. Cut into 12 equal
pieces. Shape three-quarters of each piece into a ball
and place in the prepared moulds. With a floured finger,
press a hole in the centre of each. Shape the remaining
pieces of dough into little plugs and press into the
holes, flattening the top slightly.

3 Place the moulds on a baking sheet, cover lightly with
oiled clingfilm and let stand in a warm place for 1 hour,
until the dough comes almost to the top.

4 Brush the brioches with beaten egg and bake in
a preheated oven, 220°C/425°F/Gas Mark 7, for
15 minutes, or until golden brown. Serve warm with
butter, if you like.

date & honey loaf

ingredients

serves 10

butter, for greasing
250 g/9 oz strong white bread
    flour, plus extra for dusting
75 g/2¾ oz strong brown
    bread flour
½ tsp salt
1 sachet easy-blend dried yeast
200 ml/7 fl oz lukewarm water
3 tbsp corn oil
3 tbsp honey
75 g/2¾ oz dried dates, chopped
2 tbsp sesame seeds

method

1 Grease a 900-g/2-lb loaf tin with butter. Sift the white and brown flours into a large bowl and stir in the salt and yeast. Pour in the water, oil and honey and mix to form a dough.

2 Place the dough on a lightly floured work surface and knead for 5 minutes, or until smooth, then place in a greased bowl. Cover and let rise in a warm place for 1 hour, or until doubled in size.

3 Knead in the dates and the sesame seeds. Shape the dough and place in the prepared loaf tin. Cover and let stand in a warm place for a further 30 minutes, or until springy to the touch.

4 Bake the loaf in a preheated oven, 220°C/425°F/ Gas Mark 7, for 30 minutes, or until the bottom of the loaf sounds hollow when tapped. Transfer to a wire rack and cool completely. Serve cut into thick slices.

mango twist bread

ingredients

makes 1 loaf

3 tbsp butter, diced, plus extra
for greasing
450 g/1 lb strong white bread
flour, plus extra for dusting
1 tsp salt
1 sachet easy-blend
dried yeast
1 tsp ground ginger
50 g/1¾ oz brown sugar
1 small mango, peeled, pitted and
blended to a purée
250 ml/9 fl oz lukewarm water
2 tbsp honey
125 g/4½ oz sultanas
1 egg, beaten lightly
icing sugar, for dusting

method

1 Grease a baking sheet with a little butter. Sift the flour and salt into a mixing bowl, stir in the dry yeast, ginger and brown sugar and rub in the butter with your fingertips until the mixture resembles breadcrumbs.

2 Stir in the mango purée, lukewarm water and honey and bring together to form a dough.

3 Place the dough on a lightly floured work surface. Knead for about 5 minutes, until smooth. Alternatively, use an electric mixer with a dough hook. Place the dough in a greased bowl, cover and let rise in a warm place for about 1 hour, until it has doubled in size.

4 Knead in the sultanas and shape the dough into 2 rope shapes, each 25 cm/10 inches long. Carefully twist the 2 pieces together and pinch the ends to seal. Place the dough on the baking sheet, cover and let stand in a warm place for a further 40 minutes.

5 Brush the loaf with the egg. Bake in a preheated oven, 220°C/425°F/Gas Mark 7, for 30 minutes, or until golden. Cool on a wire rack and dust with icing sugar before serving.

black olive focaccia

ingredients

serves 12

500 g/1 lb 2 oz strong white bread
    flour, plus extra for dusting
1 tsp salt
2 tsp easy-blend dried yeast
350 ml/12 fl oz tepid water
6 tbsp extra-virgin olive oil, plus
    extra for brushing
115 g/4 oz pitted black olives,
    coarsely chopped
1 tsp rock salt

method

1 Sift the flour and salt into a warmed bowl and stir in the
yeast. Pour in the water and 2 tablespoons of the olive
oil and mix to a soft dough. Knead the dough on a
lightly floured work surface for 5–10 minutes, or until
it becomes smooth and elastic. Transfer it to a clean,
warmed, oiled bowl and cover with clingfilm. Let stand
in a warm place for 1 hour, or until the dough has
doubled in size.

2 Brush 2 baking sheets with oil. Punch the dough to
knock out the air, then knead on a lightly floured work
surface for 1 minute. Add the olives and knead until
combined. Divide the dough in half, shape into 2 oval
shapes 28 x 23 cm/11 x 9 inches long and place on the
prepared baking sheets. Cover with oiled clingfilm and
let stand in a warm place for 1 hour, or until the dough
is puffy.

3 Press your fingers into the dough to make dimples,
drizzle over 2 tablespoons of oil, and sprinkle with
the rock salt. Bake in a preheated oven, 200°C/400°F/
Gas Mark 6, for 30–35 minutes, or until golden. Drizzle
with the remaining olive oil and cover with a cloth,
to give a soft crust. Slice each loaf into 6 pieces and
serve warm.

focaccia with roasted cherry tomatoes, basil & crispy pancetta

ingredients

serves 4–6

500 g/1 lb 2 oz white bread flour, plus extra for kneading and rolling
1 tbsp dried basil
½ tsp sugar
2 tsp rapid-rise dried yeast
2 tsp salt
325 ml/11 fl oz lukewarm water
2 tbsp olive oil, plus extra for oiling

topping

400 g/14 oz cherry tomatoes
1 tbsp olive oil, plus extra for oiling and drizzling
200 g/7 oz thick pancetta, diced
4 tbsp chopped fresh basil
salt and pepper

method

1 Place the flour, dried basil, sugar, yeast and salt in a bowl. Combine the water and oil and mix with the dry ingredients to form a soft dough, adding more water if the dough appears too dry. Turn out onto a lightly floured work surface and knead for 10 minutes, until smooth and elastic. Place in a lightly oiled bowl and cover with clingfilm. Let stand in a warm place for 1 hour, or until doubled in size.

2 Place the tomatoes on a baking sheet covered with baking paper, sprinkle with oil and season to taste with salt and pepper. Bake in a preheated oven, 140°C/275°F/Gas Mark 1, for 30 minutes, until soft.

3 Increase the oven temperature to 220°C/425°F/Gas Mark 7. Remove the dough from the bowl and knead again briefly. Shape into a rectangle and place on a lightly oiled baking sheet, turning the dough over to oil both sides. Make rough indentations in the dough using your fingers. Top with the tomatoes and pancetta. Sprinkle with salt and pepper. Let stand in a warm place for 10 minutes for the dough to rise again. Bake for 15–20 minutes, until golden and cooked through. Drizzle with oil and top with fresh basil. Serve warm.

olive & sun-dried tomato bread

ingredients

serves 4

400 g/14 oz plain flour, plus extra
for dusting

1 tsp salt

1 sachet easy-blend dried yeast

1 tsp brown sugar

1 tbsp chopped fresh thyme

200 ml/7 fl oz warm water (heated
to 50°C/122°F)

4 tbsp olive oil, plus
extra for oiling

50 g/1¾ oz black olives, pitted
and sliced

50 g/1¾ oz green olives, pitted and
sliced

100 g/3½ oz sun-dried tomatoes
in oil, drained and sliced

1 egg yolk, beaten

method

1 Place the flour, salt and yeast in a bowl and mix together, then stir in the sugar and thyme. Make a well in the centre. Slowly stir in enough water and oil to make a dough. Mix in the olives and sun-dried tomatoes. Knead the dough for 5 minutes, then form it into a ball. Brush a bowl with oil, add the dough and cover with clingfilm. Let rise in a warm place for about 1½ hours, or until the dough has doubled in size.

2 Dust a baking sheet with flour. Knead the dough lightly, then cut into two halves and shape into ovals or circles. Place them on the baking sheet, cover with clingfilm and let rise again in a warm place for 45 minutes, or until they have doubled in size.

3 Make 3 shallow diagonal cuts on the top of each piece of dough. Brush with the egg. Bake in a preheated oven, 200°C/400°F/Gas Mark 6, for 40 minutes, or until cooked through – they should be golden on top and sound hollow when tapped on the bottom. Transfer to wire racks to cool. Store in an airtight container for up to 3 days.

cheese & chive plait

ingredients

serves 10

450 g/1 lb strong white bread
    flour, plus extra for dusting
1 tsp salt
1 tsp caster sugar
1½ tsp easy-blend dried yeast
2 tbsp butter
115 g/4 oz coarsely grated
    Cheddar cheese
3 tbsp snipped fresh chives
4 spring onions, chopped
150 ml/5 fl oz tepid milk
175 ml/6 fl oz tepid water
vegetable oil, for brushing
beaten egg, for glazing

method

1 Sift the flour and salt into a warmed bowl and stir in
    the sugar and yeast. Rub in the butter, then stir in the
    cheese, chives and spring onions. Make a well in the
    centre. Mix together the milk and water, pour into the
    well and mix to make a soft dough. Turn the dough
    out onto a lightly floured work surface and knead for
    10 minutes, or until smooth and elastic.

2 Transfer the dough to a clean, oiled bowl and cover
    with clingfilm. Let stand in a warm place for 1 hour, or
    until doubled in size. Brush a large baking sheet with
    oil. Turn the dough out onto a floured work surface and
    knead for 1 minute. Divide the dough into 3 pieces. Roll
    out each piece into a rope shape and plait the 3 pieces
    together, pinching the ends to seal.

3 Place on the prepared baking sheet and cover with
    oiled clingfilm. Stand in a warm place for 45 minutes,
    or until doubled in size. Brush with beaten egg and
    bake in a preheated oven, 220°C/425°F/Gas Mark 7, for
    20 minutes.

4 Reduce the temperature of the oven to 180°C/350°F/
    Gas Mark 4 and bake for a further 15 minutes, or until
    golden brown and the loaf sounds hollow when
    tapped on the bottom. Serve warm or cold.

turkish flatbread

ingredients

serves 8

750 g/1 lb 10 oz plain flour,
    plus extra for dusting
1½ tsp salt
1 tsp ground cumin
½ tsp ground coriander
1 tsp caster sugar
7 g/¼ oz easy-blend dried yeast
2 tbsp olive oil, plus extra
    for brushing
400 ml/14 fl oz lukewarm water

method

1 Sift the flour, salt, cumin and coriander together into a bowl and stir in the sugar and yeast. Make a well in the centre and pour in the oil and lukewarm water. Stir well with a wooden spoon until the dough begins to come together, then knead with your hands until it leaves the side of the bowl. Turn out onto a lightly floured surface and knead well for about 10 minutes, until smooth and elastic.

2 Brush a bowl with oil. Shape the dough into a ball, put it in the bowl and cover with a damp tea towel. Leave to rise in a warm place for 1 hour, until the dough has doubled in volume. Lightly brush a baking tray with oil. Turn out the dough onto a lightly floured surface, knock back with your fist and knead for 1–2 minutes. Divide the dough into eight equal pieces, shape each piece into a ball, then roll out to a 20-cm/8-in round. Cover the rounds with a damp tea towel and leave to rest for 20 minutes.

3 Heat a heavy-based frying pan and brush the base with oil. Add one dough round, cover and cook for 2–3 minutes, until lightly browned on the underside. Turn over with a fish slice, re-cover the pan and cook for a further 2 minutes, until lightly browned on the second side. Remove from the pan and cook the remaining dough rounds in the same way.

coriander & garlic naan

ingredients

serves 3

280 g/10 oz strong white flour,
    plus extra for dusting
1 tsp salt
1 tbsp ground coriander
1 garlic clove, very finely chopped
1 tsp easy-blend dried yeast
2 tsp clear honey
100 ml/3½ fl oz lukewarm water
4 tbsp natural yogurt
1 tbsp vegetable oil, plus extra
    for brushing
1 tsp black onion seeds
1 tbsp chopped fresh coriander

method

1 Sift the flour, salt and ground coriander together into a bowl and stir in the garlic and yeast. Make a well in the centre and pour in the honey, water, yogurt and oil. Stir well with a wooden spoon until the dough begins to come together, then knead with your hands until it leaves the side of the bowl. Turn out onto a lightly floured surface and knead well for about 10 minutes, until smooth and elastic.

2 Brush a bowl with oil. Shape the dough into a ball, put it in the bowl and cover with a damp tea towel. Leave to rise in a warm place for 1–2 hours, until the dough has doubled in volume. Oil three baking trays and place in a preheated oven, 240°C/475°F/Gas Mark 9. Turn out the dough and knock back with your fist. Divide the dough into three pieces. Shape each piece of dough into a ball and cover two dough pieces with oiled clingfilm.

3 Roll out the uncovered piece of dough into a teardrop shape about 8 mm/³⁄₈ inch thick and cover with oiled clingfilm. Roll out the other pieces of dough in the same way. Place the naan on the preheated baking trays and sprinkle with the onion seeds and chopped coriander. Bake for 5 minutes, until puffed up. Transfer the naan bread to the grill pan, brush with oil and grill for 2–3 minutes. Serve warm.

bagels

ingredients

serves 10

350 g/12 oz strong white flour,
　　plus extra for dusting
2 tsp salt
7 g/¼ oz easy-blend dried yeast
1 tbsp lightly beaten egg
200 ml/7 fl oz lukewarm water
vegetable oil, for brushing
1 egg white
2 tsp water
2 tbsp caraway seeds

method

1 Sift the flour and salt together into a bowl and stir in
the yeast. Make a well in the centre, pour in the egg
and the lukewarm water and mix to a dough. Turn out
onto a lightly floured surface and knead until smooth.

2 Brush a bowl with oil. Shape the dough into a ball,
place it in the bowl and cover with a damp tea towel.
Leave to rise in a warm place for 1 hour, until the dough
has doubled. Brush two baking trays with oil and dust
with flour. Turn out the dough and knock back. Knead
for 2 minutes, then divide into ten pieces. Shape each
piece into a ball and leave to rest for 5 minutes. Flatten
each ball and make a hole in the centre. Put on the tray,
cover and leave to rise in a warm place for 20 minutes.

3 Bring a large saucepan of water to the boil. Reduce the
heat to a simmer, then add two bagels. Poach each pair
for 1 minute, turn over and poach for a further 30
seconds. Remove with a slotted spoon and drain.

4 Transfer the bagels to the prepared baking trays. Beat
the egg white with the water in a bowl and brush it
over the bagels. Sprinkle with the caraway seeds and
bake in a preheated oven, 220°C/425°F/Gas Mark 7, for
25–30 minutes, until golden brown. Transfer to a wire
rack to cool.

english muffins

ingredients

serves 10–12

2 x 7-g/¹/₄-oz sachets
    easy-blend dried yeast
250 ml/9 fl oz tepid water
125 ml/4 fl oz natural yogurt
450 g/1 lb strong plain flour
¹/₂ tsp salt
50 g/1³/₄ oz fine semolina
vegetable oil, for greasing
butter and jam (optional), to serve

method

1 Mix the yeast with half the tepid water in a bowl until it has dissolved. Add the remaining water and the yogurt and mix well.

2 Sift the flour into a large bowl and add the salt. Pour in the yeast liquid and mix well to a soft dough. Turn out onto a floured work surface and knead well until very smooth. Place in the bowl, cover with clingfilm and let rise for 30–40 minutes in a warm place until it has doubled in size.

3 Turn out again onto the work surface and knead lightly. Roll out the dough to a thickness of 2 cm/ ³/₄ inch. Using a 7.5-cm/3-inch cutter, cut into rounds and scatter the semolina over each muffin. Re-roll the trimmings of the dough and make further muffins until it is all used up. Place them on a lightly floured baking sheet, cover and let rise again for 30–40 minutes.

4 Heat a large frying pan and lightly grease with a piece of scrunched-up kitchen paper dipped in vegetable oil. Cook half the muffins for 7–8 minutes on each side, taking care not to burn them. Repeat with the rest of the muffins. Serve at once with lots of butter and jam, if liked.

cheese & tomato pizza

ingredients

serves 2

dough

225 g/8 oz plain flour, plus extra
    for dusting

1 tsp salt

1 tsp easy-blend dried yeast

1 tbsp olive oil, plus extra
    for brushing

6 tbsp lukewarm water

topping

6 tomatoes, sliced thinly

175 g/6 oz mozzarella cheese,
    drained and sliced thinly

2 tbsp shredded fresh basil leaves

2 tbsp olive oil

salt and pepper

method

1 To make the pizza dough, sift the flour and salt into a
    bowl and stir in the yeast. Make a well in the centre and
    pour in the oil and water. Gradually incorporate the dry
    ingredients into the liquid, using a wooden spoon or
    floured hands.

2 Turn out the dough onto a lightly floured work surface
    and knead well for 5 minutes, until smooth and elastic.
    Return to the clean bowl, cover with lightly oiled
    clingfilm and set aside to rise in a warm place for
    about 1 hour, or until doubled in size.

3 Turn out the dough onto a lightly floured work surface
    and knock down. Knead briefly, then cut it in half and
    roll out each piece into a circle about 5 mm/¼ inch
    thick. Transfer to a lightly oiled baking sheet and push
    up the edges with your fingers to form a small rim.

4 For the topping, arrange the tomato and mozzarella
    slices alternately over the pizza bases. Season to taste
    with salt and pepper, sprinkle with the basil and drizzle
    with the olive oil. Bake in a preheated oven, 230°C/
    450°F/Gas Mark 8, for 15–20 minutes, until the crust is
    crisp and the cheese has melted. Serve immediately.

blinis

ingredients

serves 8

115 g/4 oz buckwheat flour
115 g/4 oz white bread flour
7-g/¼-oz sachet easy-blend
 dried yeast
1 tsp salt
375 ml/13 fl oz tepid milk
2 eggs, 1 whole and
 1 separated
vegetable oil, for brushing
soured cream and smoked
 salmon, to serve

method

1 Sift both flours into a large, warmed bowl. Stir in the yeast and salt. Beat in the milk, whole egg and egg yolk until smooth. Cover the bowl and let stand in a warm place for 1 hour.

2 Place the egg white in a spotlessly clean bowl and whisk until soft peaks form. Fold into the batter. Brush a heavy-based frying pan with oil and set over medium–high heat. When the frying pan is hot, pour enough of the batter onto the surface to make a blini about the size of a saucer.

3 When bubbles rise, turn the blini over with a spatula and cook the other side until light brown. Wrap in a clean tea towel to keep warm while cooking the remainder. Serve the warm blinis with soured cream and smoked salmon.

savoury
nibbles

savoury oat crackers

ingredients

serves 12–14

100 g/3½ oz unsalted butter,
    plus extra for greasing
90 g/3¼ oz rolled oats
25 g/1 oz wholemeal flour
½ tsp coarse sea salt
1 tsp dried thyme
40 g/1½ oz walnuts,
    finely chopped
1 egg, beaten
40 g/1½ oz sesame seeds

method

1 Lightly grease two baking trays.

2 Rub the butter into the oats and flour, using your fingertips. Stir in the salt, thyme and walnuts, then add the egg and mix to a soft dough. Spread out the sesame seeds on a large shallow plate or tray. Break off walnut-sized pieces of dough and roll into balls, then roll in the sesame seeds to coat lightly and evenly.

3 Place the balls of dough on the prepared baking trays, spacing well apart, and roll the rolling pin over them to flatten as much as possible. Bake in a preheated oven, 180°C/350°F/Gas Mark 4, for 12–15 minutes, or until firm and pale golden.

4 Cool on the baking trays for 3–4 minutes, then transfer to a wire rack to finish cooling.

cheese & mustard scones

ingredients

serves 8

50 g/1¾oz butter, diced,
    plus extra for greasing
225 g/8 oz self-raising flour,
    plus extra for dusting
1 tsp baking powder
pinch of salt
125 g/4½ oz mature Cheddar
    cheese, grated
1 tsp mustard powder
150 ml/5 fl oz milk, plus extra
    for brushing
pepper

method

1 Lightly grease a baking tray.

2 Sift the flour, baking powder and salt into a mixing bowl. Rub in the butter with your fingertips until the mixture resembles breadcrumbs.

3 Stir in the cheese, mustard and enough milk to form a soft dough.

4 On a lightly floured surface, knead the dough very lightly, then flatten it out with the palm of your hand to a depth of about 2.5 cm/1 inch.

5 Cut the dough into eight wedges with a knife. Brush each one with a little milk and sprinkle with pepper to taste.

6 Bake in a preheated oven, 220°C/425°F/Gas Mark 7, for 10–15 minutes, until golden brown. Transfer the scones to a wire rack and leave to cool slightly before serving.

quiche lorraine

ingredients

serves 4

pastry
200 g/7 oz plain flour,
  plus extra for dusting
100 g/3½ oz salted butter
1–2 tbsp cold water

filling
15 g/½ oz butter
1 small onion, finely chopped
4 lean streaky bacon rashers, diced
55 g/2 oz Gruyère cheese or
  Cheddar cheese, grated
2 eggs, beaten
300 ml/10 fl oz single cream
pepper

method

1 For the pastry, sift the flour into a bowl and rub in the butter with your fingertips until the mixture resembles fine breadcrumbs. Stir in just enough water to bind the mixture to a firm dough.

2 Roll out the dough on a lightly floured surface to a round slightly larger than a 23-cm/9-inch loose-based tart tin, 3 cm/1¼ inches deep. Lift the pastry onto the tin and press it down into the fluted edge. Trim off the excess pastry. Prick the base all over with a fork. Chill to allow the pastry to rest and prevent shrinkage.

3 Place a sheet of baking paper in the pastry-lined tin. Fill with baking beans and bake in a preheated oven, 200°C/400°F/Gas Mark 6, for 10 minutes. Remove the paper and beans and bake for a further 10 minutes.

4 For the filling, melt the butter in a frying pan and cook the onion and bacon until soft and lightly browned. Spread in the hot pastry case and sprinkle with half the cheese. Beat the eggs and cream and season to taste. Pour into the pastry case and sprinkle with cheese.

5 Reduce the oven temperature to 190°C/375°F/ Gas Mark 5. Place the quiche in the oven and bake for 25–30 minutes, or until golden brown and just set. Cool for 10 minutes before turning out.

goat's cheese & thyme tart

ingredients

serves 6

250 g/9 oz ready-made puff pastry

topping

500 g/1 lb 2 oz goat's cheese,
    such as chèvre, sliced
3–4 sprigs fresh thyme, leaves
    picked from stalks
55 g/2 oz black olives, pitted
50 g/1¾ oz tinned anchovies
    in olive oil
1 tbsp olive oil
1 egg yolk
salt and pepper
sprigs of fresh thyme, to garnish

method

1 Roll the dough into a large circle or rectangle and place
    on a baking sheet.

2 Arrange the cheese slices on the dough, leaving a
    2.5-cm/1-inch margin round the edge. Sprinkle the
    thyme and olives, then arrange the anchovies, over the
    cheese. Drizzle over the olive oil. Season well with salt
    and pepper and brush the edges of the dough with
    the egg yolk.

3 Bake in a preheated oven, 190°C/375°F/Gas Mark 5, for
    20–25 minutes, until the cheese is bubbling and the
    pastry is browned. Garnish with sprigs of fresh thyme.

crab & watercress tart

ingredients

serves 6

pastry

125 g/4½ oz plain flour

pinch of salt

75 g/2½ oz cold butter,
    cut into pieces, plus extra
    for greasing

cold water

filling

300 g/10½ oz prepared white and
    brown crabmeat

1 bunch watercress, washed and
    leaves picked from stems

50 ml/2 fl oz milk

2 large eggs, plus 3 egg yolks

200 ml/7 fl oz double cream

½ tsp ground nutmeg

½ bunch fresh chives, snipped

2 tbsp finely grated Parmesan
    cheese

salt and pepper

fresh sprigs of watercress,
    to garnish

method

1 Lightly grease a 23-cm/9-inch loose-based fluted tart
tin. Sift the flour and salt into a food processor, add
the butter and process until the mixture resembles fine
breadcrumbs. Add just enough cold water to bring the
dough together.

2 Turn out onto a floured work surface and roll out the
dough 8 cm/3¼ inches larger than the tin. Lift the
dough into the tin and press to fit. Neaten and trim the
edges. Fit a piece of baking paper into the tart case, fill
with dried beans and chill for 30 minutes.

3 Remove the pastry case from the refrigerator and bake
blind for 10 minutes in a preheated oven, 190°C/375°F/
Gas Mark 5. Return to the oven for 5 minutes. Remove
the tin from the oven and lower the oven temperature
to 160°C/325°F/Gas Mark 3.

4 Arrange the crabmeat and watercress in the tart tin.
Whisk the milk, eggs and egg yolks together in a bowl.
Simmer the cream in a pan and pour over the egg
mixture, whisking all the time. Season with salt, pepper
and nutmeg and stir in the chives. Carefully pour this
mixture over the crab and watercress and sprinkle over
the Parmesan. Bake for 35–40 minutes, until golden
and set. Let the tart stand for 10 minutes before
serving, garnished with sprigs of watercress.

triple tomato tart

ingredients

serves 6

250 g/9 oz ready-made puff pastry

topping

3 tbsp sundried tomato paste
250 g/9 oz ripe vine tomatoes, sliced
150 g/5½ oz cherry tomatoes, cut in half
2 sprigs fresh rosemary
2 tbsp extra-virgin olive oil
1 tbsp balsamic vinegar
1 egg yolk
125 g/4½ oz Italian sliced salami, chopped
salt and pepper
handful of thyme sprigs

method

1 Roll out the dough to form a rectangle 35 cm/14 inches long and 25 cm/10 inches wide and lift the dough onto a heavy-duty baking sheet. Spread the sundried tomato paste over the dough, leaving a 3-cm/1¼-inch margin round the edge. Arrange the vine tomato slices over the tomato paste, sprinkle over the cherry tomato halves and top with the rosemary. Drizzle with 1 tablespoon of the olive oil and the balsamic vinegar.

2 Brush the edges of the dough with the egg yolk and bake in a preheated oven, 190°C/375°F/Gas Mark 5, for 10 minutes. Sprinkle over the chopped salami and bake for a further 10–15 minutes.

3 Remove the tart from the oven and season to taste with salt and pepper. Drizzle with the remaining olive oil and sprinkle with the thyme.

spring vegetable tart

ingredients

serves 6

pastry
250 g/9 oz plain flour
pinch of salt
125 g/4½ oz cold butter,
    cut into pieces
55 g/2 oz grated Parmesan cheese
1 egg
1 tbsp cold water

filling
300 g/11 oz selection of baby
    spring vegetables, such as
    carrots, asparagus, peas, broad
    beans, spring onions, corn cobs
    and leeks, trimmed and peeled
    where necessary
300 ml/10 fl oz double cream
125 g/4½ oz mature Cheddar
    cheese, grated
2 eggs plus 3 egg yolks
handful of fresh tarragon and
    flatleaf parsley, chopped
salt and pepper

method

1 Grease a 25-cm/10-inch loose-based tart tin. Sift the flour and salt into a food processor, add the butter and pulse to combine, then tip into a large bowl and add the Parmesan cheese. Mix the egg and water together in a small bowl. Add most of the egg mixture and work into a soft dough, using more egg mixture if needed. Turn out onto a floured work surface and roll out the dough 8 cm/3¼ inches larger than the tin. Carefully lift the dough into the tin and press to fit. Trim the excess dough. Fit a piece of baking paper into the tart case, fill with dried beans and chill for 30 minutes.

2 Bake the tart case blind for 15 minutes in a preheated oven, 200°C/400°F/Gas Mark 6, then remove the beans and paper and bake for a further 5 minutes. Remove from the oven and cool. Lower the oven temperature to 180°C/350°F/Gas Mark 4.

3 Cut the vegetables into bite-sized pieces and blanch in boiling water. Drain and cool. Bring the cream to simmering point in a pan. Place the cheese, eggs and egg yolks in a heatproof bowl and pour the warm cream over the mixture. Stir to combine, season well and stir in the herbs. Arrange the vegetables in the tart case, pour over the cheese filling and bake for 30–40 minutes, until set. Cool in the tin for 10 minutes before serving.

yellow courgette tart

ingredients

serves 6

1 quantity cheese pastry

filling

2 large yellow courgettes
1 tbsp salt
3 heaped tbsp unsalted butter
1 bunch spring onions, trimmed
    and finely sliced
150 ml/5 fl oz double cream
3 large eggs
1 small bunch of fresh chives,
    chopped, plus extra to garnish
salt and white pepper

method

1 Grease a 25-cm/10-inch loose-based tart tin. Roll out the pastry 8 cm/3¼ inches larger than the tin. Carefully lift the dough into the tin and press to fit. Roll the rolling pin over the tin to neaten the edges and trim the excess dough. Fit a piece of baking paper into the tart case, fill with dried beans and chill for 30 minutes.

2 Bake the tart case blind for 15 minutes in a preheated oven, 200°C/400°F/Gas Mark 6, then remove the beans and paper and bake for a further 5 minutes. Remove from the oven and cool. Lower the oven temperature to 180°C/350°F/Gas Mark 4.

3 Meanwhile, grate the courgettes and put in a sieve with 1 tablespoon of salt. Drain for 20 minutes, then rinse and put in a clean tea towel, squeezing all the moisture from the courgettes. Keep dry.

4 Melt the butter in a wide frying pan, sauté the spring onions until soft, then add the courgettes and cook over medium heat for 5 minutes, until any liquid has evaporated. Cool slightly. Whisk the cream and eggs together with the salt and pepper and chives. Spoon the courgettes into the tart case and pour in the cream mixture, making sure it settles properly, then bake for 30 minutes. Serve the tart hot or cold, garnished with fresh chives.

squash, sage & gorgonzola tart

ingredients

serves 6

1 quantity pastry

filling

½ small butternut squash or
    1 slice pumpkin, weighing
    250 g/9 oz
1 tsp olive oil
250 ml/9 fl oz double cream
175 g/6 oz Gorgonzola cheese
2 eggs, plus 1 egg yolk
6–8 fresh sage leaves
salt and pepper

method

1 Cut the squash in half and brush the cut side with the oil. Place cut-side up on a baking sheet and bake for 30–40 minutes, until browned and very soft. Set aside to cool. Remove the seeds and scoop out the flesh into a large bowl, discarding the skin.

2 Lightly grease a 23-cm/9-inch loose-based fluted tart tin. Roll out the pastry 8 cm/3¼ inches larger than the tin. Lift the dough into the tin and press to fit. Roll the rolling pin over the tin to trim the excess dough. Fit a piece of baking paper into the tart case and fill it with dried beans. Chill in the refrigerator for 30 minutes, then bake blind for 10 minutes in a preheated oven, 190°C/375°F/Gas Mark 5. Remove the beans and paper and return to the oven for 5 minutes.

3 Mash the squash and mix it with half the cream, season with salt and pepper, then spread it in the pastry case. Slice the cheese and lay it on top. Whisk the remaining cream with the eggs and egg yolk and pour the mixture into the tart tin, making sure it settles evenly. Arrange the sage leaves in a circle on the surface. Bake for 30–35 minutes and leave for 10 minutes in the tin before serving.

artichoke & pancetta tartlets

ingredients

serves 6

butter, for greasing
flour, for dusting
1 quantity pastry

filling

5 tbsp double cream
4 tbsp bottled artichoke paste
400 g/14 oz canned artichoke
    hearts, drained
12 thin-cut pancetta slices
rocket leaves
50 g/1¾ oz Parmesan or
    pecorino cheese
2 tbsp olive oil, for drizzling
salt and pepper

method

1 Grease 6 x 9-cm/3½-inch loose-based fluted tart tins.
Divide the pastry into 6 pieces. Roll each piece to fit the
tart tins. Carefully fit each piece of dough in its tin and
press well to fit. Roll the rolling pin over the tin to trim
the excess dough. Cut 6 pieces of baking paper and fit
a piece into each tart, fill with dried beans and chill in
the refrigerator for 30 minutes.

2 Bake the tart cases for 10 minutes in a preheated oven,
200°C/400°F/Gas Mark 6, and then remove the beans
and baking paper.

3 Meanwhile, stir the cream and the artichoke paste
together and season well with salt and pepper. Divide
between the pastry cases, spreading out to cover
the base of each tart. Cut each artichoke heart into
3 pieces and divide between the tarts, curl 2 slices of
the pancetta into each tart and bake for 10 minutes.

4 To serve, top each tart with a good amount of rocket
then, using a potato peeler, sprinkle shavings of the
Parmesan cheese over the tarts, drizzle with olive oil
and serve at once.

smoked salmon, dill & horseradish tartlets

ingredients

serves 6

1 quantity pastry

filling

125 ml/4 fl oz soured cream
1 tsp creamed horseradish
½ tsp lemon juice
1 tsp Spanish capers, chopped
3 egg yolks
200 g/7 oz smoked salmon
trimmings
bunch fresh dill, chopped
salt and pepper

method

1 Grease 6 x 9-cm/3½-inch loose-based fluted tart tins. Divide the pastry into 6 pieces. Roll each piece to fit the tart tins. Carefully fit each piece of dough in its tin and press well to fit. Roll the rolling pin over the tin to trim the excess dough. Cut 6 pieces of baking paper and fit a piece into each tart, fill with dried beans and chill in the refrigerator for 30 minutes.

2 Bake the tart cases for 10 minutes in a preheated oven, 200°C/400°F/Gas Mark 6, and then remove the beans and baking paper.

3 Meanwhile, put the soured cream, horseradish, lemon juice, capers and salt and pepper into a bowl and mix. Add the egg yolks, the smoked salmon and the dill and carefully mix again. Divide this mixture between the tart cases and return to the oven for 10 minutes. Cool in the tins for 5 minutes before serving.

feta & spinach tartlets

ingredients

serves 6

1 quantity pastry
   with ½ nutmeg, freshly grated,
   added to the flour

filling

225 g/8 oz baby spinach
2 tbsp butter
150 ml/5 fl oz double cream
3 egg yolks
125 g/4½ oz Feta cheese
25 g/1 oz pine nuts
salt and pepper
cherry tomatoes and sprigs of
   flat-leaf parsley, to garnish

method

1 Grease 6 x 9-cm/3½-inch loose-based fluted tart tins.
   Divide the pastry into 6 pieces. Roll each piece to fit the
   tart tins. Carefully fit each piece of dough in its tin and
   press well to fit. Roll the rolling pin over the tin to trim
   the excess dough. Cut 6 pieces of baking paper and fit
   a piece into each tart, then fill with dried beans and
   chill in the refrigerator for 30 minutes.

2 Bake the tart cases for 10 minutes in a preheated oven,
   200°C/400°F/Gas Mark 6, and then remove the beans
   and baking paper.

3 Blanch the spinach in boiling water for just 1 minute,
   then drain and press to squeeze all the water out. Chop
   the spinach. Melt the butter in a frying pan, add the
   spinach and cook gently to evaporate any remaining
   liquid. Season well with salt and pepper. Stir in the
   cream and egg yolks. Crumble the feta and divide
   between the tarts, top with the creamed spinach and
   bake for 10 minutes. Sprinkle the pine nuts over the
   tartlets and cook for a further 5 minutes.

4 Garnish with cherry tomatoes and sprigs of flat-leaf
   parsley.

potato & pancetta muffins

ingredients

serves 12

1 tbsp sunflower or peanut oil,
   plus extra for oiling
   (if using)
3 shallots, finely chopped
350 g/12 oz self-raising flour
1 tsp salt
450 g/1 lb potatoes, cooked
   and mashed
2 large eggs
350 ml/12 fl oz milk
125 ml/4 fl oz soured cream
1 tbsp finely snipped
   fresh chives
150 g/5½ oz pancetta, grilled
   and crumbled into pieces
4 tbsp grated Cheddar cheese

method

1 Oil a 12-cup muffin tin with sunflower oil, or line it with 12 muffin paper liners. Heat the remaining oil in a frying pan, add the chopped shallots and cook, stirring, over low heat for 2 minutes. Remove from the heat and cool.

2 Sift the flour and salt into a large mixing bowl. In a separate bowl, mix together the mashed potatoes, eggs, milk, soured cream, chives and half of the pancetta. Add the potato mixture to the flour mixture and then gently stir together until just combined. Do not overstir the batter – it is fine for it to be a little lumpy.

3 Divide the muffin batter evenly between the 12 cups in the muffin tin or the paper liners (they should be about two-thirds full). Sprinkle over the remaining pancetta, then sprinkle over the grated Cheddar cheese. Transfer to a preheated oven, 200°C/400°F/Gas Mark 6, and bake for 20 minutes, or until risen and golden. Remove the muffins from the oven and serve warm, or place them on a wire rack to cool.

herb muffins with smoked cheese

ingredients

serves 12

1 tbsp sunflower or peanut oil, for oiling (if using)

280 g/10 oz plain flour

2 tsp baking powder

½ tsp baking soda

25 g/1 oz smoked hard cheese, grated

50 g/1¾ oz fresh parsley, finely chopped

1 large egg, lightly beaten

300 ml/10 fl oz thick strained plain yogurt

4 tbsp butter, melted

method

1 Oil a 12-cup muffin tin with sunflower oil, or line it with 12 muffin paper liners. Sift the flour, baking powder and baking soda into a large mixing bowl. Add the smoked cheese and the parsley and mix together well.

2 In a separate bowl, lightly mix the egg, yogurt and melted butter together. Add the yogurt mixture to the flour mixture and then gently stir together until just combined. Do not overstir the batter – it is fine for it to be a little lumpy.

3 Divide the muffin batter evenly between the 12 cups in the muffin tin or the paper liners (they should be about two-thirds full), then transfer to a preheated oven, 200°C/400°F/Gas Mark 6. Bake for 20 minutes, or until risen and golden. Remove the muffins from the oven and serve warm, or place them on a wire rack to cool.

soured cream muffins with chives

ingredients

serves 12

1 tbsp sunflower or peanut oil,
    for oiling (if using)
280 g/10 oz plain flour
2 tsp baking powder
½ tsp baking soda
25 g/1 oz Cheddar cheese, grated
35 g/1¼ oz fresh chives, finely
    snipped, plus extra to garnish
1 large egg, lightly beaten
200 ml/7 fl oz soured cream
100 ml/3½ fl oz plain
    unsweetened yogurt
4 tbsp butter, melted

method

1 Oil a 12-cup muffin tin with sunflower oil, or line it with 12 muffin paper liners. Sift the flour, baking powder and baking soda into a large mixing bowl. Add the cheese and chives and mix together well.

2 In a separate bowl, lightly mix the egg, soured cream, yogurt and melted butter together. Add the soured cream mixture to the flour mixture and then gently stir together until just combined. Do not overstir the batter – it is fine for it to be a little lumpy.

3 Divide the muffin batter evenly between the 12 cups in the muffin tin or the paper liners (they should be about two-thirds full). Sprinkle over the remaining snipped chives to garnish and transfer to a preheated oven, 200°C/400°F/Gas Mark 6. Bake for 20 minutes, or until risen and golden. Remove the muffins from the oven and serve warm, or place them on a wire rack to cool.

cheese & rosemary sables

ingredients

serves 40

225 g/8 oz cold butter, diced,
    plus extra for greasing
250 g/9 oz plain flour
250 g/9 oz grated Gruyère cheese
½ tsp cayenne pepper
2 tsp finely chopped fresh
    rosemary leaves
1 egg yolk, beaten with
    1 tbsp water

method

1 Lightly grease 2 baking sheets. Place the flour, butter, cheese, cayenne pepper and chopped rosemary in a food processor. Pulse until the mixture forms a dough, adding a little cold water, if necessary, to bring the mixture together.

2 On a floured work surface, roll out the dough to 5 mm/¼ inch thick. Stamp out shapes such as stars and hearts with 6-cm/2½-inch biscuit cutters.

3 Place the shapes on the prepared baking sheets, then cover with clingfilm and chill in the refrigerator for 30 minutes, or until firm. Brush with the beaten egg yolk and bake in a preheated oven, 180°C/350°F/Gas Mark 4, for 10 minutes, or until golden brown. Cool on the baking sheets for 2 minutes, then serve warm or transfer to wire racks to cool.

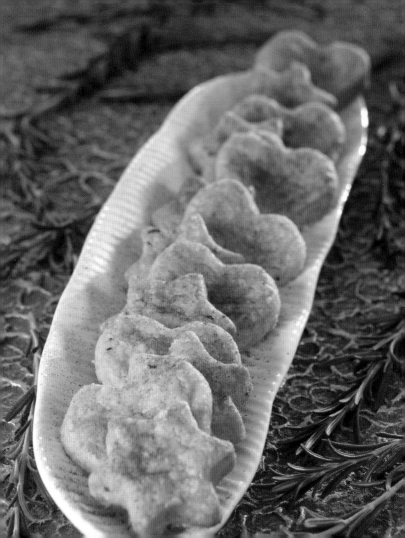

pesto palmiers

ingredients

serves 20

butter, for greasing
plain flour, for dusting
250 g/9 oz ready-made
    puff pastry
3 tbsp green or red pesto
1 egg yolk, beaten with
    1 tbsp water
25 g/1 oz freshly grated
    Parmesan cheese
sprigs of fresh basil, to garnish

method

1 Grease a baking sheet with a little butter. On a floured work surface, roll out the pastry to a 35 x 15-cm/ 14 x 6-inch rectangle and trim the edges with a sharp knife. Spread the pesto evenly over the pastry. Roll up the ends tightly to meet in the centre of the pastry.

2 Wrap in clingfilm and chill in the refrigerator for 20 minutes, until firm, then remove from the refrigerator and unwrap. Brush with the beaten egg yolk on all sides. Cut across into 1-cm/½-inch thick slices. Place the slices on the prepared baking sheet.

3 Bake in a preheated oven, 200°C/400°F/Gas Mark 6, for 10 minutes, or until crisp and golden. Remove from the oven and immediately sprinkle over the Parmesan cheese. Serve the palmiers warm or transfer to a wire rack and cool to room temperature. Garnish with sprigs of fresh basil.

cheese straws

ingredients

serves 24

115 g/4 oz plain flour, plus extra
    for dusting
pinch of salt
1 tsp curry powder
55 g/2 oz butter, plus extra
    for greasing
55 g/2 oz grated Cheddar cheese
1 egg, beaten
poppy and cumin seeds,
    for sprinkling

method

1 Sift the flour, salt and curry powder into a bowl.
   Add the butter and rub in until the mixture resembles
   breadcrumbs. Add the cheese and half the egg and mix
   to form a dough. Wrap in clingfilm and chill in the
   refrigerator for 30 minutes.

2 Lightly grease several baking sheets. On a floured
   work surface, roll out the dough to 5-mm/¼-inch thick.
   Cut into 7.5 x 1-cm/3 x ½-inch strips. Pinch the strips
   lightly along the sides and place on the prepared
   baking sheets.

3 Brush the straws with the remaining egg and sprinkle
   half with poppy seeds and half with cumin seeds.
   Bake in a preheated oven, 200°C/400°F/Gas Mark 6,
   for 10–15 minutes, or until golden. Transfer to wire
   racks to cool.

index